# The Literary Journal in America, 1900-1950

**AMERICAN LITERATURE, ENGLISH LITERATURE, AND WORLD LITERATURES IN ENGLISH: AN INFORMATION GUIDE SERIES**

Series Editor: Theodore Grieder, Division of Special Collections, Fales Library, New York University, New York, New York

Associate Editor: Duane DeVries, Assistant Professor, Polytechnic Institute of New York, Brooklyn, New York

*Other books on American literature in this series:*

THE LITERARY JOURNAL IN AMERICA TO 1900—*Edited by Edward E. Chielens*

LITTLE MAGAZINES IN AMERICA, 1950-1975—*Edited by Robert Bertholf**

AMERICAN FICTION TO 1900—*Edited by David K. Kirby*

AMERICAN FICTION, 1900-1950—*Edited by James Woodress*

CONTEMPORARY FICTION IN AMERICA AND ENGLAND, 1950-1970—*Edited by Alfred F. Rosa and Paul A. Echholz*

AFRO-AMERICAN FICTION—*Edited by Edward Margolies and David Bakish**

AMERICAN DRAMA TO 1900—*Edited by Walter J. Meserve**

AMERICAN DRAMA, 1900-1950—*Edited by Paul Hurley**

CONTEMPORARY DRAMA IN AMERICA AND ENGLAND, 1950-1970—*Edited by Richard H. Harris**

AMERICAN PROSE AND CRITICISM TO 1820—*Edited by Donald Yannella and John Roch**

AMERICAN PROSE AND CRITICISM, 1820-1900—*Edited by Elinore H. Patridge**

AMERICAN PROSE AND CRITICISM, 1900-1950—*Edited by Peter A. Brier**

AMERICAN POETRY TO 1900—*Edited by Bernice Slote**

AMERICAN POETRY, 1900-1950—*Edited by William White and Artem Lozynsky**

AFRO-AMERICAN POETRY AND DRAMA—*Edited by William French, Geneviève E. and Michel Fabre, and Amritjit Singh**

* in preparation

---

The above series is part of the

**GALE INFORMATION GUIDE LIBRARY**

The Library consists of a number of separate series of guides covering major areas in the social sciences, humanities, and current affairs.

General Editor: Paul Wasserman, Professor and former Dean, School of Library and Information Services, University of Maryland

Managing Editor: Denise Allard Adzigian, Gale Research Company

# The Literary Journal in America, 1900-1950

## A GUIDE TO INFORMATION SOURCES

---

*Volume 16 in the American Literature, English Literature, and World Literatures in English Information Guide Series*

**Edward E. Chielens**

*Chairman, Department of English and Speech*
*Detroit College of Business*

***Gale Research Company***
*Book Tower, Detroit, Michigan 48226*

**Library of Congress Cataloging in Publication Data**

Chielens, Edward E
The literary journal in America, 1900-1950.

(American literature, English literature, and world literatures in English ; v. 16)
Includes index.
1. American periodicals--History--Bibliography. 2. American literature--Periodicals--History--Bibliography. I. Title.
Z6951.C572 [PN4877] 016.051 74-11534
ISBN 0-8103-1240-9

To my wife
CAROLE

# VITA

Edward E. Chielens is currently chairman of the Department of English and Speech at the Detroit College of Business. He received his B.A. and Ph.D. from Wayne State University and his M.A. from the University of Michigan.

Chielens has contributed to the journals CRITICISM and GENRE. His bibliography THE LITERARY JOURNAL IN AMERICA TO 1900 was published by Gale Research Company in 1975.

# CONTENTS

# Contents

# Chapter 1
# INTRODUCTION

## IDEALISM AND CAUSES: THE LITTLE MAGAZINES

A major characteristic of twentieth-century literary journalism has been the proliferation of periodicals espousing a wide variety of aesthetic philosophies, political ideologies, regional loyalties, or the ideas of small groups of writers and poets. A similar diversity of outlook did occur among journals in the nineteenth century, primarily in the sectional rivalries and in the New York literary wars described by Perry Miller in THE RAVEN AND THE WHALE: THE WAR OF WORDS AND WITS IN THE ERA OF POE AND MELVILLE.[1] However, nothing in that century equals the burst of activity that occurred in the years following the appearance of the MASSES in New York in 1911, and POETRY in Chicago in 1912. The literary experimentation of the 1920's, and then of the Great Depression, brought forth a great number of these noncommercial, often short-lived publications which declared and defended, often arrogantly, the beliefs of their founders. Their editors heaped scorn upon the older, established journals, the ATLANTIC, HARPER'S, and the CENTURY, often considering them to be the toadies of the field, fostering mediocrity for middle America, and stifling true creativity by denying an outlet for the new, vital literature. These new journals have been called "little magazines," although the term is necessarily imprecise because of the very lack of uniformity which characterizes them. Frederick J. Hoffman, Charles Allen, and Carolyn F. Ulrich, in THE LITTLE MAGAZINE: A HISTORY AND A BIBLIOGRAPHY, the most thorough study of the subject, focus on noncommercial, avant-garde, "tendenz" journals, meaning those espousing specific literary outlooks or theories.[2] In 1948, however, two years after their work appeared, Paul Bixler challenged their use of the term. He felt that journals not purely literary should be included, and stated, "It is characteristic of the authors that they chose the year and the appearance of POETRY rather than of THE MASSES to fix the movement."[3] Jack Lindeman, editor of WHETSTONE, later formulated another characteristic which helps to define the little magazine, this time without exclusion of those publications whose interests are not purely literary. "The little mag," he states, "operates strictly according to the personal tastes and prejudices of the editor or editors implying a 'take it or leave it' concern for its audience."[4]

Often the appearance of these journals was accompanied by statements of idealistic programs and grandiose schemes, and often they quickly faded into oblivion because of financial collapse, editorial disorganization, or disinterest on the part of either potential subscribers or even the editorial staff themselves. An example is the expensively printed and high-quality journal FIRE, founded in 1926 by a group of black writers, including Langston Hughes and Zora Thurston, as an outlet for the work of what has since been called the Harlem Renaissance. But they underestimated expenses, were unable to sell many copies, and could not pay the printer's bills. For three or four years after the only issue of FIRE had come and gone, the printer attached the paychecks of Wallace Thurman, the only member of the group with a steady job. Langston Hughes later related, "Finally, irony of ironies, several hundred copies of FIRE were stored in the basement of an apartment where an actual fire occurred and the bulk of the whole issue was burned up. Now FIRE is a collector's item, and very difficult to get, being mostly ashes."[5] Thurman's later activities may serve as an example of the disillusionment that accompanies such frustrated enterprises--and attached paychecks. Hughes says that "later Thurman became a ghost writer for TRUE STORY MAGAZINE and other publications, writing under all sorts of fantastic names like Ethel Belle Mandrake or Patrick Casey. He turned out Irish and Jewish and Catholic 'True Confessions.' . . . Later he ghosted books. It has been said that he wrote blond Peggy Hopkins Joyce's 'Men, Women, and Checks.'"[6] Nevertheless, the disastrous career of FIRE is not remarkable in the field of literary journalism.

The frustrating combination of idealism and impracticality is evident in the career of Lawrence C. Woodman, who founded, edited, and mimeographed LITERARY ARTS, AMERICAN SCENE, IDIOM, and WOMANKIND in the 1930's, and in addition helped David Ignatow pay for and publish Ignatow's own ANALYTIC. In 1965 Ignatow discussed Woodman's career, his plans, and his goals in two articles in the CARLETON MISCELLANY. Ignatow stated that "in his magazines Woodman hoped to bridge the gap between the two most important trends in American writing at this time. He wanted from THE ANVIL and the NEW MASSES angry concern with the economic plight and isolation of the American worker and farmer, and from the more urbane magazines, such as the ATLANTIC, their sense of style."[7] He "was strongly opposed to the bland, pragmatic-transcendental pap published regularly then in the ATLANTIC, HARPER'S and other magazines," and he criticized the lack of literary artistry in the radical journals.[8] However, Woodman's "idealistic Herculean ambition . . . unfortunately went to prove his inability to realize it," for he attempted to edit and publish all of his short-lived journals simultaneously on the income from a WPA teaching job, and at the same time to support a wife and daughter. Ignatow concluded that Woodman's idealism and ambition were not exceptional in the 1930's: "Many of these mimeographed or hand-set magazines were being subsidized out of the Home Relief pennies of men and women determined to see that their case was put before the world. These crudely printed issues were the training ground for some of the finest writers of today."[9]

## REGIONALISM AND LITERARY PERIODICALS

Regional loyalty has been a major impetus for the founding of literary periodicals, just as it was for many periodicals in the nineteenth century. The Boston DIAL, the SOUTHERN LITERARY MESSENGER, and the OVERLAND MONTHLY are well-known examples of this earlier sectional identification. In the 1880's, however, this sectional identification declined as periodicals of national circulation, with sophisticated methods of distribution and national advertising, such as the CENTURY, began to dominate the field. The ATLANTIC, at first a periodical of New England, became national in focus under the guidance of William Dean Howells in the 1870's, and the OVERLAND MONTHLY, at one time the outlet for Bret Harte's local color fiction, after a long and checkered career "lost its larger regional tone, and with it, its real value."[10] By 1900 the major journalistic conflict was not sectional in orientation. The "quality" journals, the CENTURY, the ATLANTIC, HARPER'S, and SCRIBNER'S, all national in scope and all based in the East, were struggling against the so-called cheap magazines, such as McCLURE'S and MUNSEY'S, which effectively combined good fiction and the exciting reporting of the muckraking era. These "cheap" magazines were, in fact, able to challenge the older journals precisely because of their own sophisticated methods of national circulation and mass advertising. It was not until 1915 that regionalism began again to be asserted in literary journals, this time for reasons different from those found earlier. Writers, poets, and scholars with regional loyalties and interests resented the domination by New York, or Eastern, periodicals and publishers. Some feared the growing homogeneousness of American culture which threatened the extinction of valuable cultural differences.

Much of this regional sentiment was expressed in the South, where post-Civil War literary journals such as the SOUTHERN BIVOUAC and the SUNNY SOUTH had long since disappeared. In 1920 H.L. Mencken published a scathing attack on the South in his PREJUDICES, SECOND SERIES, entitled "The Sahara of the Bozart," and the reaction of the Southern press clearly indicated that a raw nerve had been touched.[11] Mencken said, among other things, that "in all that gargantuan paradise of the fourth-rate there is not a single picture gallery worth going into, or a single orchestra capable of playing the nine symphonies of Beethoven, or a single opera house, or a single theater devoted to decent plays. . . ."[12] Almost in reaction to Mencken's attack, a number of literary journals were founded in the South in the early 1920's. Some, like the PHOENIX of Emory University, referred to Mencken by name and claimed to be "an oasis" in the desert. An Atlanta little magazine was dubbed BOZART.[13] Fred Hobson has remarked that "after 'The Sahara of the Bozart' Mencken became, as Emily Clark of the REVIEWER described him, a 'state of mind,' and that state of mind represented not only a critical examination of the Southern tradition but even an outright rejection of certain elements of that tradition."[14]

The two most important of these regional journals were the DOUBLE DEALER, started in New Orleans in 1921 by Julius Weis Friend, Basil Thompson, and John McClure, and the REVIEWER, founded in the same year by the Virginia Writers' Club of Richmond, both with the intention of fostering creative writing in the South. The editors of the DOUBLE DEALER had originally been planning a magazine of local satire, but after Mencken's attack they altered their plans and produced a journal of Southern literature that in its five-year career provided an outlet for the work of such young writers as William Faulkner, Allen

Tate, and Ernest Hemingway, thus defying the Southern sentimental belles lettres tradition.[15] One editor declared that they would also "thereby . . . disprove H.L. Mencken's unfair blanket indictment of the South as 'the Sahara of the Bozart.'"[16] The REVIEWER, under the editorship of Emily Clark, published Southern writers and some Northern writers as well, gaining national attention in its brief five-year career. Emily Clark noted in an early editorial, "We received both scolding and petting in larger measure than we had dreamed of. . . ."[17]

However, ironies do occur in this burst of journalistic activity. For one thing, the regional orientation is not always as clearly seen in the journals' contents as it is in their editorial statements. Emily Clark was confronted with the problem of whether to publish well-known writers from other regions when she had the opportunity, or restrict the journal to obscure local authors and poets, thus lowering the REVIEWER's literary quality. She declared, somewhat unconvincingly, that the prominent writers were "bait" to attract the new writers, since payment for contributions had to be "in fame not specie."[18] Mencken himself, an enthusiastic supporter of the new enterprise and frequent correspondent with editor Clark, tried to goad her into excluding Northern writers from the journal's pages and attack the old Southern tradition more aggressively. "Its peril," he said, "is that it may sink into the puerile literary formalism that already curses the South, and so disappear beneath a sea of sweetened bilge."[19]

Mencken's interest in the REVIEWER, and in fact in the DOUBLE DEALER as well, demonstrates a second irony. Often the most enthusiastic supporters of regional literary journals were the Easterners against whom they were supposed to be rebelling. There could be danger in this development. Hobson notes, "As editor of the SMART SET and then of the AMERICAN MERCURY, Mencken undoubtedly had some interest in the REVIEWER as a proving ground for new writers whom he could later use in his own magazines."[20] Hobson quotes France Newman, a southern writer associated with the REVIEWER, who said, "One might suspect that Mr. Mencken farmed out prominent young writers to THE REVIEWER just as Mr. [John J.] McGraw farms out promising young pitchers to Minneapolis and Birmingham and then brings them back to his 'Mercury' when they are sufficiently experienced."[21] The regional journals thus could conceivably remain subordinate to the established publishers in spite of themselves.

Regional loyalties inspired the editors of literary journals in the Midwest during the same years, and they often viewed Eastern publishers in the same way that Southern editors did. John T. Frederick founded the MIDLAND in Iowa City in 1915; Harold G. Merriam founded the FRONTIER at the University of Montana in 1920; and Lowry Wimberly began the PRAIRIE SCHOONER at the University of Nebraska in 1925. The FRONTIER absorbed the MIDLAND in 1933. The three editors, because of their common interest in promoting regional writers and publishing literature with a rural orientation, maintained a cordial relationship and close communication. The NEW YORKER's initial declaration in 1925 that the NEW YORKER was "not for the old lady in Dubuque" might epitomize the Eastern attitude against which the midwestern editors felt a common resentment. In his first editorial, in the January 1915 MIDLAND, Frederick made a comparison that implicitly reveals this feeling: "Scotland is none the worse for Burns and Scott, none the worse that they did not move to London and interpret London themes for London publishers."[22] Five years later he points out that midwestern writers "have had to seek publication away from home. A result has seemed to be a tendency to false emphasis, distortion, in literary interpretations. . . . New England or California or Scotland might have been less adequately and helpfully interpreted if London had selected all writings in English that were to appear in print."[23] Consequently, Frederick took pride in the number of MIDLAND stories reprinted in Edward O'Brien's AMERICAN BEST SHORT STORIES, and in O'Brien's praise for the high quality of the journal's fiction.[24] This praise demonstrated to him the ability of his journal to stand up to national standards. Frederick published the work of Ruth Suckow, Raymond Weeks, James T. Farrell, and Edwin Ford Piper, among other midwesterners.

These journals did experience problems typical of those faced by other regional journals. For example, in spite of the quality of the MIDLAND, Frederick constantly had to plead for financial support and seek an adequate number of subscribers. In a plea for subscribers in 1931, two years before he ceased publication, Frederick wrote hopefully, "I still believe that there must be five or ten thousand people in the country who would value the MIDLAND."[25] August Derleth's statement that "the fate of creative writing in the Middle West still hangs in the balance" seems ironic in retrospect. Frederick moved the MIDLAND to Chicago, where he gave it up in 1933. In addition, the MIDLAND began to exhibit the tendency seen in the REVIEWER, to include an increasing number of writers from other regions. In the last years, when his journal became better known, though no more successful financially, Frederick received more contributions from other areas of the country, and thus published more of them. As a result, the MIDLAND's focus became less regional.[26]

The PRAIRIE SCHOONER also experienced difficulty getting local subscribers. In his study THE PRAIRIE SCHOONER STORY: A LITTLE MAGAZINE'S FIRST 25 YEARS, Paul Stewart notes that even on the University of Nebraska campus "students whose natural curiosity had been fueled . . . and who had therefore bought a copy or two of the early SCHOONER apparently decided that it was too 'literary' for their tastes."[27] Although the PRAIRIE SCHOONER has been one of the most successful and long-lived regional journals, editor Wimberly had to struggle against such indifference to keep it going. Frequently he had to depend on private donations in the early years of the SCHOONER's existence, even though he did receive a small amount of financial support from the university.

The TEXAS REVIEW, an early regional journal founded in 1915 at the University of Texas, followed a different editorial policy from those of the publications just discussed. Throughout the editorship of Robert Adger Law, and then after 1924, when the journal was moved to Southern Methodist University and became the SOUTHWEST REVIEW, a policy was consistently maintained of balancing regional and national, or international material. In the journal's fortieth anniversary issue in 1955, Lon Tinkle stated the editorial formula in this way:

"Never formulated into a program or a manifesto or a credo, this perception of a culture unique to the Southwest but kin to the parent-spirit of true culture everywhere prevailed for two decades at least in the REVIEW's policy."[28] The regional element, stated in an initial editorial by Stark Young in 1915 entitled "Reeking of the Soil," was never diminished. However, this review was not strictly a journal of creative literature, but included a substantial amount of criticism and scholarship; and this, plus the fact that it was supported by its universities and run by the resident academics, probably made it less difficult to sustain than an independent journal such as the MIDLAND, financially insecure, seeking new regional literature from obscure writers, and needing to discover good quality work in order to survive.

On the other hand, another successful Western publication, the ROCKY MOUNTAIN REVIEW, started as the INTERMOUNTAIN REVIEW in 1936 and changed to the WESTERN REVIEW in 1946, experienced more difficulty maintaining its regional focus. Editor Ray B. West was more exclusively interested in publishing literature than he was in publishing scholarship. As was the case with other regionalist editors, he encountered a lack of enthusiasm on the part of local readers, while Eastern readers and writers expressed a surprising interest in his journal. He found it necessary in 1943 to respond in an editorial to complaints that the ROCKY MOUNTAIN REVIEW was not regional enough. He declared, "A tabulation of all material published in the Review during 1942 shows that more than 50 per cent was written by Rocky Mountain authors. . . ."[29] In an earlier editorial he mildly chided local readers by noting that for every new local subscriber he got two from the East, and that New York City was second only to Salt Lake City in number of readers of the REVIEW.[30] Twice he called for subsidization of regional periodicals around the country by their local universities, probably because he was encountering financial problems.

All of these editors, and others not mentioned here, were dedicated to promoting their regions' literature and writers, and to this end they worked long hours with little or no pay. They faced a dilemma, however, for if they managed to overcome apathy and guide their periodicals to success, that success often resulted from the support of people in other regions, especially the East, either in the form of subscriptions or high-quality literary contributions. Thus, success might mean the loss of the very identity for which a journal was originally founded. Apparently, and ironically, their original resentment of the power of the Eastern literary establishment was often based on an accurate perception.

## POLITICAL FACTIONALISM AND LITERARY PERIODICALS

A second major impetus for the founding of literary journals was political idealism and loyalty. The large number of periodicals mentioned in chapter 6, "Politically Radical Literary Periodicals," indicates that often political orientation was closely related to literary interests. Unlike regionalism, this phenomenon had no close parallel in nineteenth-century literary journalism. However, like regionalism, it could cause problems and controversies, in the relationships of one journal to another and among members of the same editorial staff. The period of greatest political interest and controversy in literary journalism was the 1930's. The Great Depression radicalized many writers, and the increased concern among them for politics and social causes paralleled, and in fact caused, a similar orientation in the journals.

The NEW MASSES, founded in 1926, was the leading radical literary periodical at that time, and was backed by the Communist party. Consequently, its editors launched attacks on other left-wing literary journals they considered revisionist or "bohemian." They attacked Max Eastman and the long-defunct MASSES, which he edited from 1911 to 1917, declaring that the journal had been bohemian, smacked of Greenwich Village art rebellion, and had never lived up to its revolutionary goals. Eastman replied in two articles which appeared in the MODERN MONTHLY in 1934. He viewed the charge as absurd, and the claim that "the editors of THE NEW MASSES by contrast are carrying forward the banner of proletarian revolution . . . a piece of fabricated ballyhoo from start to finish."[31] Mike Gold, who had made similar accusations while on the MASSES editorial staff, had become an editor of the NEW MASSES, and probably was instrumental in these criticisms of Eastman. It might seem absurd that the NEW MASSES editors would even bother to criticize the policies of a periodical which had been ended over ten years before. But the MASSES had a reputation which bordered on the legendary, for its editors and artists had been brought to trial by the U.S. government twice for crusading against involvement in World War I, and the journal had been the outlet for the writings of John Reed, who had been closely associated with its editors. Reed was viewed by many leftist writers as an awesome and heroic figure because of his courage and his early death in Russia. Also, the writers and artists of the MASSES often took an ironic or humorous view of American culture and politics. Even its successor the LIBERATOR, founded by the same group after the suppression of the MASSES and lasting until 1924, was more serious in tone. Richard Fitzgerald has, in fact, seen the difference as part of a long-term change, for he has stated that "compared with the MASSES, the LIBERATOR reflected the process of transition between the latitudinarian, ideologically vague, and Village-oriented American socialism of the pre-Russian Revolution years and the hard-line communism of the depression."[32] The editors of the NEW MASSES were much more serious, and humorless, in following their editorial policies. Fitzgerald suggests that, as a result, they were much less successful than their predecessors of the MASSES in publishing exciting and high-quality art and literature.[33] Thus the attitude expressed in the later journal toward its predecessor was not based on petty jealousy or a conflict of editors' personalities; it was part of a long-term gradual change of outlook and emphasis which had occurred between 1917 and the Depression.

The MODERN MONTHLY, which had served as the vehicle for Eastman's replies to the NEW MASSES, was itself repeatedly criticized by that periodical. Its editor, V.F. Calverton, was one of the maverick leftist editors of the 1920's and 1930's, as was Jack Conroy, founder of the ANVIL and the NEW ANVIL. Calverton ran his journal from 1923 to 1940, defying these attacks and promoting black radical literature. The MODERN MONTHLY, entitled the MODERN QUARTERLY from 1923 to 1932, and 1938 to 1940, survived his death by only one issue. Conroy edited three journals in the 1930's, the REBEL POET from

1931 to 1932, the ANVIL from 1932 until it was taken over by the PARTISAN REVIEW in 1935, and the NEW ANVIL from 1939 to 1940. He also maintained a running feud with the Communist party which, he claimed, engineered the end of the first ANVIL because of his independent spirit. The combined ANVIL AND PARTISAN REVIEW, Conroy later said, provided the party with space for "the dialectical gymnastics so dear to the hearts of the New York intelligentsia. . . ."[34] He founded the NEW ANVIL with Nelson Algren, who had also disapproved of the earlier merger with the PARTISAN REVIEW. Although these editors expressed basically similar views of American society and its economic system, and they all promoted proletarian literature, their feuds were as passionate as any in the field of literary journalism.

The one radical literary publication to survive this period is the PARTISAN REVIEW, perhaps because of its editors' ability to change policy at the right times. In fact, its radicalism has diminished over the years, and in 1963 it was even institutionalized at Rutgers University. Its first editors, William Phillips and Philip Rahv, broke with the Communist party because of Stalinism and suspended publication in the fall of 1936, resuming publication the next year. They were attacked by the NEW MASSES on the one hand, and on the other Malcolm Cowley in the NEW REPUBLIC accused them of a narrow Trotskyist viewpoint.[35] But the magazine survived these criticisms, becoming less political and more established. In 1956, expressing both admiration and exasperation for the PARTISAN REVIEW, Leslie Fiedler observed, "Blasted into ashes by its enemies, mourned prematurely by its friends, despaired of by its own editors--it yet somehow survives; and that is, after all, the point."[36] Survival may in this case have resulted from mutability. As I have noted earlier, idealism, especially when coupled with impracticality, has been the cause of the early death of many a literary journal.

Political factors have also influenced the histories of journals which were not politically oriented, most notably the SEVEN ARTS. Founded in 1916 by James Oppenheim on a subsidy from Mrs. A.K. Rankine, the SEVEN ARTS displayed an impressive list of contributors and subeditors, including Waldo Frank, Randolph Bourne, Van Wyck Brooks, and Lewis Mumford. The journal promoted American literature and art and called for an independence from European culture. But when Bourne wrote pacifist articles for the periodical urging America to remain neutral in the war, social pressure was brought upon Mrs. Rankine; she withdrew the subsidization, and publication of the SEVEN ARTS was stopped.[37] In his MEMOIRS Waldo Frank called this quick end "The Tragedy of the SEVEN ARTS," and said that the tragedy was the direct result of the war or wartime politics and social pressures. He concludes that the editors' unwillingness or inability to compromise was the ultimate cause of the loss of the periodical: "If we editors had known our creation, perhaps we would have been inspired to transcend our egos, to study this storm of war, to learn how to survive it."[38] This cause of the journal's demise is particularly remarkable since the SEVEN ARTS was not primarily a political publication. Bourne voiced the same opinions about the war in the DIAL, at that time under Martyn Johnson's editorship.[39] Nicholas Joost has noted that in response the DIAL "first persecuted and drove away its most brilliant voice only to admit later that Randolph Bourne had been right after all."[40] The views of the war expressed in the DIAL were thus embarrassingly confusing and contradictory. The journal was delivered from its plight when Scofield Thayer and James Sibley Watson took it over and transformed it into a totally apolitical avant-garde little magazine of art and literature. It fared much better in the literary controversies of the 1920's than it did earlier in political ones. On the whole, however, the political factor has played a remarkably important role in the history of modern literary journalism.

## EDITORIAL POLICIES OF LITTLE MAGAZINES

The third major reason for the founding of literary periodicals has been the development of various literary theories and causes by groups of writers and individuals, especially in the 1920's. Little magazines served as outlets for these theories and supportive literature. However, they varied widely in the extent to which they narrowly adhered to one viewpoint, some being more anthological than programmatic. Gorham Munson, editor of the journal SECESSION from 1922 to 1924, felt that the effectiveness of a periodical could be impaired if its editorial policies were at either extreme, too narrow on the one hand or too broad and directionless on the other. He considered Margaret Anderson's LITTLE REVIEW, run according to her own personal tastes and even whims, to be an example of the first, and BROOM to be an example of the second. The proper passage between "Scylla and Charybdis," he said, was the one followed by his own journal, which "aims to be neither . . . but a group organ."[41] The group SECESSION represented were the new, little-known writers--quite a large group of diverse talents and tastes, after all, and one which many little magazines claimed to represent.

Other magazinists have also commented on which of these editorial policies is most effective. Reviewing new little magazines in POETRY in 1948, William Van O'Connor stated, "That many little magazines have survived only a very short time may in part be the result of each of them trying to reach the same audience."[42] By narrowing their editorial interests, O'Connor maintained, journals could avoid this competition and accomplish more than they would by attempting merely to publish the best fiction, poetry, and criticism available. An exchange of attitudes on this issue appeared in the PRAIRIE SCHOONER in 1939. Author Weldon Kees lamented the disappearance of almost all of the radical little magazines devoted to left-wing literature, including FRONT, LEFT, the ANVIL, BLAST, and others. He felt that the loss should be remedied by the establishment of a periodical "appearing regularly and often enough, devoted chiefly to creative work, with metropolitan aims. . . ."[43] But an editorial reply in the same issue took exception to these views. The editors noted that among the journals which had survived for many years, the SOUTHWEST REVIEW, the FRONTIER-MIDLAND, and the PRAIRIE SCHOONER all had the benefits of being associated with universities. They went on to note, however:

> Another fact that may explain the longevity of these publications is that no one of them is, or ever has been, an experimental magazine. And that they are not experimental is in their favor. The experimentalist always has an axe to grind--the left-wing axe, the

> agrarian axe, or some other kind of axe. And as a consequence, he is, nine times out of ten, a poser and a dishonest writer.[44]

Indeed, the less experimental journals, those with the broadest editorial policies, have had a better survival rate. This may, in fact, be the major reason why the PARTISAN REVIEW outlasted the radical publications mentioned by Kees. On the other hand, longevity clearly cannot be the only measurement of success or effectiveness. The oldest remaining periodicals in this bibliography are the ATLANTIC and HARPER'S, and these are among the publications, whatever their merits, which stood for the literary establishment against which journals such as the MIDLAND placed themselves. In an article on experimental, program-oriented little magazines, Felix Pollak has stated, "In their light, there is cause for the hope that the minimal, the individual, the spiritual anti-body, as it were, will always again assert and reassert itself, the multiform forever rebel against the uniform, counteracting every substandard standardization."[45]

TRANSITION is one of these experimental and relatively short-lived little magazines with specific editorial programs, and its history shows that success means more than survival. Eugene Jolas founded TRANSITION in 1927, in order to express his revolutionary literary theories and publish literature which supported or exemplified them. He rebelled against descriptive naturalism. Language, he felt, should be reformed into a new idiom which would reflect the subtleties of the human psyche or the subconscious. As a result, he was at first sympathetic to dadaism and surrealism. Then he espoused a new theory called vertigralism, "the intuitive reaching toward the above," toward the "man who will participate in the collective consciousness of the universe, who will find contact with the . . . world soul."[46] As one might expect, much of TRANSITION's contents were close to the incomprehensible. Jolas expected no large following, nor did he receive one. Nevertheless, Lincoln Kirstein noted in his own journal, HOUND & HORN, that TRANSITION was an important publication: "Unwieldy, non-selective, printing much that has little or no value, and very little that can have any claims to permanence, it is nevertheless an invaluable organ."[47] Jolas was the first to introduce surrealism to American readers, and his journal published in serial form James Joyce's new project called "Work in Progress," later entitled FINNEGAN'S WAKE. To Jolas, Joyce's writing exemplified the "Revolution of the Word" for which he was fighting. Jolas and others associated with TRANSITION in fact helped Joyce with his revising and rewriting before each installment, since the writer's eyesight was failing. Very few, if any, longer-lived, more broadly based journals can claim a more important share in the development of modern literature than can this highly experimental periodical.

## MAJOR WRITERS AND LITERARY PERIODICALS

The most important role of literary periodicals in this century has been their relationship to writers who are now considered among the best in the field. Journals often served either as training grounds in the early careers of such men and women, or else provided outlets, and thus encouragement, for their work when the commercial press was not interested in them. TRANSITION's role in this regard has already been noted. POETRY, the LITTLE REVIEW, and the DIAL under Thayer and Watson are other excellent examples. Harriet Monroe, founder and editor of POETRY in Chicago in 1912, championed the imagists and other new poets while, as Charles Allen has noted, the established periodicals, such as the ATLANTIC and HARPER'S MONTHLY, were publishing traditional, vapid poetry, almost all of which was deservedly destined for obscurity.[48] Ezra Pound sent T.S. Eliot's "The Love Song of J. Alfred Prufrock" to Monroe, and in his collected LETTERS is a communication urging her to publish it.[49] She finally agreed, and this central document in modern literary history first appeared in her journal. Pound also served as a liaison for the LITTLE REVIEW when he was its London editor, most notably for the publication of Joyce's ULYSSES in installments in the journal, incidentally much to the chagrin of the post office, which took Margaret Anderson to court under the obscenity laws. In fact, critic Ruthven Todd considered Pound to have been instrumental in making the LITTLE REVIEW one of the important journals of the century, for before 1917 it was only "a scrappy repository for anything that happened to appeal to Margaret Anderson, showing neither editorial standards nor a balanced point of view."[50] Pound eventually fell out with Anderson because she refused to guarantee publication of his, Eliot's, Joyce's, and Wyndham Lewis's work.

The DIAL, one of the most ably produced journals of the period, in terms of its editing and printing, published the work of many important writers, its policies showing surprising diversity. For example, it was a strong force in developing interest in primitive art, for it reproduced examples of Southwest American Indian art and poetry in its pages. It provided an outlet for D.H. Lawrence's work in America, including fiction, nonfiction, and poetry. In 1921 Sherwood Anderson received the DIAL Award, and in 1922 it was given to T.S. Eliot, whose "Waste Land" first appeared in the DIAL. In exasperation at the choice of Anderson, Gorham Munson wrote in his journal SECESSION, "It would be less compromising to go one way or the other. Stay on dry land like the ATLANTIC MONTHLY or leap headfirst into the contemporary stream."[51] The DIAL's policies also exasperated Ernest Hemingway, whose contributions in the early 1920's were repeatedly rejected. He apparently harbored resentment against the journal and Gilbert Seldes, one of its editors, long after he became an established writer. Hemingway may have purposely distorted his discussion of Ernest Walsh in "The Man Who Was Marked for Death," a chapter in A MOVEABLE FEAST, in order to cast aspersion on the DIAL and its policies. Walsh's writings, according to this account, may have received special consideration by DIAL editors. The specifics of Hemingway's relationship with the journal have been studied and debated by Nicholas Joost and William Wasserstrom, both scholars of the DIAL's history.[52] It is certain, however, that the DIAL was prestigious enough to cause Hemingway deep and lasting disappointment when its editors refused his work.

Although less well known than the three periodicals discussed above, the FUGITIVE served as an important outlet for the early work of Allen Tate, John Crowe Ransom, Donald Davidson, and Robert Penn Warren, members of the literary group associated with Vanderbilt University in Nashville which founded the journal in 1922. They met regularly, read and discussed each other's poetry, and published it in their periodical. They rejected the old Southern literary tradition and developed their own views of poetry and the relationship of the artist to his culture. John M. Bradbury, in THE FUGITIVES: A CRITICAL ACCOUNT, notes that as time went on, "the enthusiastic unanimity of its beginning had been dissipated, but the cofraternity of its editors had never been broken. Ideologically and artistically they were taking different directions, asserting individualities which generally had been submerged in the group effect."[53] In 1925 publication of the journal was suspended, as each went his own way, some to involvement with other literary journals. In his biography of Allen Tate, Radcliffe Squires observed that "Warren would take to THE SOUTHERN REVIEW; Ransom to THE KENYON REVIEW; and Tate to THE SEWANEE REVIEW. In this way THE FUGITIVE rose from its ashes to continue in the most powerful and sensitive voices in American culture for a span of three decades."[54] Even though the FUGITIVE lasted only a short time, and did not achieve the reputation of other journals, it performed an important role in the history of American literary journalism, as a training ground both for writers and for future editors of other, more prominent publications.

Literary journals performed this function from early in the century through the 1940's. For example, William Marion Reedy, editor of REEDY'S MIRROR in St. Louis, offered advice and encouragement to Edgar Lee Masters, and in the May 29, 1914, issue of the MIRROR he began serial publication of SPOON RIVER ANTHOLOGY. He also offered advice and encouragement to Theodore Dreiser, who often sought Reedy's advice and faithfully read the MIRROR throughout its publishing career from 1893 to 1920.[55] William Carlos Williams was one of a number of writers and poets who also served as editors. He has said of CONTACT, the short-lived and nearly forgotten periodical he founded in 1921 with Robert McAlmon, that "Hemingway's earliest short stories, even before the Paris days, would not have been possible without the CONTACT backing and my own SPRING AND ALL owes its appearance solely to CONTACT."[56] The importance of little magazines in Hemingway's early career, especially the DOUBLE DEALER, POETRY, the LITTLE REVIEW, and THIS QUARTER, is shown in Nicholas Joost's detailed study, ERNEST HEMINGWAY AND THE LITTLE MAGAZINES: THE PARIS YEARS.[57] Periodicals thus have fostered the work of young writers since before 1920, when Harry T. Baker stated in the NORTH AMERICAN REVIEW that "periodicals may be said to have fostered the growth of permanent literature,"[58] through the 1940's, when, for example, Whit and Hallie Burnett's STORY published fiction by Norman Mailer and Truman Capote.

The sources of information on literary journals in America tell an interesting, important, and at times even dramatic story. That story includes accounts of jury trials, for obscenity in the cases of Margaret Anderson's LITTLE REVIEW and H.L. Mencken's AMERICAN MERCURY, and for conspiracy against the government in the case of the MASSES. It includes the careers of editors whose policies and personalities have made them more written about and wondered at than most writers. One of these was Harold Ross, who founded and successfully established the NEW YORKER, but whose bizarre methods, such as removing an employee's office furniture and equipment piece by piece in order to fire him, made him a curiosity from the beginning. Much has also been written about H.L. Mencken, whose editorial work on the SMART SET and the AMERICAN MERCURY has drawn nearly as much interest from scholars as has his writing. Most important, however, this story shows that literary journals and their editors, for the most part ignored by students of literature, have played an indispensable role in the development of modern American letters.

## THE BIBLIOGRAPHY: SCOPE AND LIMITATIONS

I have followed the same guidelines for determining which publications to include in this bibliography that I followed in THE LITERARY JOURNAL IN AMERICA TO 1900. I have included those in which literature--fiction, poetry, and philosophical, critical, or familiar essays--was a primary element. I have defined and included as journals and periodicals publications appearing no more frequently than once a week, no more infrequently than twice a year. This yardstick eliminates both daily and yearly publications, including yearbooks and newspapers. Also, I have included individual sections only on those journals which have been the subject of books, chapters in books, or articles. A number of other periodicals, though not literary under my definition, have published significant literary material, among them the NATION and the NEW REPUBLIC. I have not compiled a bibliography of the secondary sources concerning these publications, since many of these sources do not deal with literary matters. Instead, I have included an appendix of material dealing with only the literary aspects of these journals.

Sections on individual journals have been placed within chapters according to the journal's nature or type, in order to present a clearer picture of the entire field of literary journalism. At times this was difficult, as in the case of the FUGITIVE, which might be considered a regional publication. In such cases I have relied on internal evidence, the opinions or attitudes of the editors, and the views of scholars who have written about the journals, in order to place them appropriately in the bibliography.

Some of the journals included here were founded before 1900 or published beyond 1950. As a general rule, however, I have included only those entries which focus on this fifty-year time period.

# NOTES: INTRODUCTION

1. Perry Miller, THE RAVEN AND THE WHALE: THE WAR OF WORDS AND WITS IN THE ERA OF POE AND MELVILLE (New York: Harcourt, Brace, 1956).

2. Frederick J. Hoffman, Charles Allen, and Carolyn F. Ulrich, THE LITTLE MAGAZINE: A HISTORY AND A BIBLIOGRAPHY (1946; rpt. New York: Kraus Reprint, 1967).

3. Paul Bixler, "Little Magazine, What Now?" ANTIOCH REVIEW, 8 (1948), 63.

4. Jack Lindeman, Untitled article, MAINSTREAM, 15 (December 1962), 37.

5. Langston Hughes, "Harlem Literati in the Twenties," SATURDAY REVIEW OF LITERATURE, 22 June 1940, p. 14.

6. Ibid., p. 13.

7. David Ignatow, "Unfinished Business," CARLETON MISCELLANY, 6 (Winter 1965), 70.

8. Ibid., p. 69.

9. Ibid., p. 74.

10. Goldie Capers Smith, "THE OVERLAND MONTHLY: Landmark in American Literature," NEW MEXICO QUARTERLY, 33 (1963), 339. See also Van Wyck Brooks, HOWELLS: HIS LIFE AND WORLD (New York: E.P. Dutton, 1959), pp. 91-92.

11. Fred C. Hobson, Jr., SERPENT IN EDEN: H.L. MENCKEN AND THE SOUTH (Chapel Hill: University of North Carolina Press, 1974), pp. 26-28.

12. H.L. Mencken, "The Sahara of the Bozart," PREJUDICES: SECOND SERIES (New York: Alfred A. Knopf, 1920), p. 138.

13. Hobson, p. 54.

14. Hobson, p. 32.

15. Frances Jean Bowen, "The New Orleans DOUBLE DEALER," LOUISIANA HISTORICAL QUARTERLY, 39 (1956), 444.

16. Hobson, p. 49.

17. Emily Clark, "At Random: Beginning the Second Volume," REVIEWER, 2 (1921), 39.

18. Emily Clark, "At Random: The Facts of the Case Are These," REVIEWER, 2 (1922), 336.

19. Quoted in Hobson, p. 39.

20. Hobson, p. 47.

21. Quoted in Hobson, p. 47.

22. John T. Frederick, Editorial, MIDLAND, 1 (1915), 1.

23. John T. Frederick, "After Five Years," MIDLAND, 6 (1920), 1.

24. Frank Luther Mott, TIME ENOUGH: ESSAYS IN AUTOBIOGRAPHY (Chapel Hill: University of North Carolina Press, 1962), p. 127.

25. Quoted in August W. Derleth, "The Plight of the MIDLAND," COMMONWEAL, 17 February 1932, p. 439.

26. Lois T. Hartley, "THE MIDLAND," IOWA JOURNAL OF HISTORY, 47 (1949), 340-41.

27. Paul Robert Stewart, THE PRAIRIE SCHOONER STORY: A LITTLE MAGAZINE'S FIRST 25 YEARS (Lincoln: University of Nebraska Press, 1955), p. 35.

28. Lon Tinkle, "Milestone for a Magazine," SOUTHWEST REVIEW, 40 (1955), 284.

29. R[ay] B. W[est], "Editorial Aims," ROCKY MOUNTAIN REVIEW, 7 (Spring-Summer 1943), 2.

30. "Stock Taking," ROCKY MOUNTAIN REVIEW, 6 (Fall 1941), 2.

31. Max Eastman, "New Masses for Old," MODERN MONTHLY, 8 (1934), 293. See also Eastman's "Bunk about Bohemia," MODERN MONTHLY, 8 (1934), 200-208.

32. Richard Fitzgerald, "MASSES: New York, 1911-1917. LIBERATOR: New York: 1918-1924," in THE AMERICAN RADICAL PRESS, 1880-1960, ed. Joseph R. Conlin (Westport, Conn.: Greenwood Press, 1974), II, 538.

33. Richard Fitzgerald, "NEW MASSES: New York, 1926-1948," THE AMERICAN RADICAL PRESS, 1880-1960, ed. Conlin, II, 545.

34. Jack Conroy, "Introduction," WRITERS IN REVOLT: THE ANVIL ANTHOLOGY, ed. Jack Conroy and Curt Johnson (New York: Lawrence Hill, 1973), p. xviii.

35. Malcolm Cowley, "PARTISAN REVIEW," NEW REPUBLIC, 19 October 1938, pp. 311-12.

36. Leslie A. Fiedler, "'Partisan Review': Phoenix or Dodo?" PERSPECTIVES USA, no. 15 (Spring 1956), p. 97.

37. James Oppenheim, "The Story of the SEVEN ARTS," AMERICAN MERCURY, 20 (1930), 164.

38. Waldo Frank, MEMOIRS OF WALDO FRANK, ed. Alan Trachtenberg (Amherst: University of Massachusetts Press, 1973), p. 95.

39. Nicholas Joost, "Culture vs. Power: Randolph Bourne, John Dewey, and THE DIAL," MIDWEST QUARTERLY, 9 (1968), 251-52.

40. Ibid., p. 257.

41. Gorham B. Munson, "Interstice between Scylla and Charybdis," SECESSION, no. 2 (July 1922), p. 32.

42. William Van O'Connor, "The Direction of the Little Magazine," POETRY, 71 (1948), 281.

43. Weldon Kees, "Magazine Chronicle," PRAIRIE SCHOONER, 13 (1939), 68.

44. L[owry] C[harles] W[imberly], "Ox Cart," PRAIRIE SCHOONER, 13 (1939), 68.

45. Felix Pollak, "Landing in Little Magazines--Capturing(?) a Trend," ARIZONA QUARTERLY, 19 (1963), 114-15.

46. Quoted in Hoffman, Allen, and Ulrich, THE LITTLE MAGAZINE: A HISTORY AND A BIBLIOGRAPHY, p. 178.

47. Lincoln Kirstein, "TRANSITION," HOUND & HORN, 2 (1929), 198.

48. Charles Allen, "American Little Magazines--POETRY: A MAGAZINE OF VERSE," AMERICAN PREFACES, 3 (1937), 28-32.

49. Ezra Pound, THE LETTERS OF EZRA POUND, 1907-1941, ed. D.D. Paige (New York: Harcourt, Brace, 1950), pp. 50-51.

50. Ruthven Todd, "THE LITTLE REVIEW," TWENTIETH CENTURY VERSE, no. 15-16 (February 1939), p. 159.

51. Gorham Munson, "Expose No. 1," SECESSION, no. 1 (Spring 1922), p. 23.

52. Nicholas Joost, "Ernest Hemingway and THE DIAL," NEOPHILOLOGUS, 5 (1968), 189-90, 304-13; William Wasserstrom, "Hemingway, the DIAL, and Ernest Walsh," SOUTH ATLANTIC QUARTERLY, 65 (1966), 171-77.

53. John M. Bradbury, THE FUGITIVES: A CRITICAL ACCOUNT (Chapel Hill: University of North Carolina Press, 1958), p. 26.

54. Radcliffe Squires, ALLEN TATE: A LITERARY BIOGRAPHY (New York: Pegasus, 1971), p. 54.

55. Max Putzel, "Dreiser, Reedy, and 'DeMaupassant, Junior,'" AMERICAN LITERATURE, 33 (1962), 466.

56. William Carlos Williams, "The CONTACT Story," CONTACT, 1, no. 1 (1959), 76.

57. Nicholas Joost, ERNEST HEMINGWAY AND THE LITTLE MAGAZINES: THE PARIS YEARS (Barre, Mass.: Barre Publishers, 1968).

58. Harry T. Baker, "Periodicals and Permanent Literature," NORTH AMERICAN REVIEW, 212 (1920), 787.

# Chapter 2

# GENERAL STUDIES AND VIEWS

[Alden, Henry Mills]. "Editor's Study." HARPER'S MONTHLY, 106 (1903), 654-56.

According to Alden the best writers willingly accept the advice of helpful magazine editors.

______. MAGAZINE WRITING AND THE NEW LITERATURE. New York: Harper and Brothers, 1908.

Chapters V through VIII discuss the American magazine and its audience. Most of the chapters in this book originated in Alden's "Editor's Study" column in HARPER'S.

Atherton, Gertrude. "Literary Merchandise." NEW REPUBLIC, 3 July 1915, pp. 233-34.

The writer decries the lack of literary quality found in the fiction of the fifteen-cent monthlies. She offers as a major reason the rejection by the public of the anemic literature of the earlier "quality" journals.

Bacon, Cleveland Frederick. "College Literature and Journalism." CRITIC, 37 (1900), 21-30.

Bacon reviews college literary publications, and concludes that the humorous periodicals contain the best material.

Bakeless, John. MAGAZINE MAKING. New York: Viking Press, 1935.

This study is intended "to give a general survey of the main problems of magazine publishing in the United States." Bakeless focuses on the problems of "quality" periodicals such as the ATLANTIC and HARPER'S. Chapters include "Economic Basis of the Magazine" (chapter I), "Editor and Author" (chapter VII), and "Book Reviews" (chapter IX).

Baker, Harry T. "Periodicals and Permanent Literature." NORTH AMERICAN REVIEW, 212 (1920), 777-87.

Baker considers the number of well-known writers who published good literature in periodicals and concludes, "Within reasonable limits, therefore, periodicals may be said to have fostered the growth of permanent literature."

Barrett, William. "Declining Fortunes of the Literary Review: 1945-57." ANCHOR REVIEW, no. 2 (1957), pp. 145-60.

The literary reviews, which in the past thrived on new ideas and experimentation, are increasingly succumbing to the conformity and institutionalization of American life. Even the "snotty young man" who once wrote for the avant-garde periodicals has retreated to the safe world of academia. "He, if anyone does, knows that Bohemia belongs to the past, that modern society has closed down on it, and that the literary review, which once drew its sustenance from that quarter, is no longer possible."

Beary, Thomas John. "Poetic Theory and Practice in THE NEW MASSES and SPIRIT, 1930-1939." Dissertation, New York University, 1950.

Beary compares the views expressed in a left-wing radical journal to those found in a Catholic journal. He concludes that two distinct poetic traditions existed in America in the 1930's, and the Marxist tradition made little permanent contribution to American poetic philosophy.

B[enet], W[illiam] R[ose]. "'Is It What Our Readers Want?'" SATURDAY PAPERS: ESSAYS ON LITERATURE FROM THE LITERARY REVIEW. THE FIRST VOLUME OF SELECTIONS FROM THE LITERARY REVIEW OF THE NEW YORK EVENING POST. New York: Macmillan, 1921, pp. 67-72.

With their concern for "the particular kind of trash that soothes without puzzling the stereotyped mind," modern periodicals, "popularly supposed to encourage creative literature," fail to fulfill their role properly.

_____. "Poetry and Periodicals." DESIGNED FOR READING: AN ANTHOLOGY DRAWN FROM THE SATURDAY REVIEW OF LITERATURE, 1924-1934. Ed. Henry Seidel Canby et al. New York: Macmillan, 1934, pp. 15-21.

Benet discusses the policies toward poetry of modern literary periodicals, using his own editorial work on the SATURDAY REVIEW OF LITERATURE as a reference.

Brown, Frederic C. "Literary Journalism in Theory and Practice." PUBLIC LIBRARIES, 13 (1908), 159-62.

Brown discusses the obstacles facing the editor of a literary journal, including an indifferent public and a scarcity of talented writers. He concludes, though, that any improvement in the quality of American scholarship will depend upon the success of such publications.

Canby, Henry Seidel. "Free Fiction." ATLANTIC, 116 (1915), 60-68.

Canby criticizes short stories published in literary and other periodicals because of their formularized, unoriginal plots and unconvincing portrayals of American life.

Churchill, Allen. THE IMPROPER BOHEMIANS: A RE-CREATION OF GREENWICH VILLAGE IN ITS HEYDAY. New York: E.P. Dutton, 1959.

Chapter IV, "The MASSES," covers the history of that periodical up to the American involvement in World War I. Chapter V, "Trials and Tribulations," discusses the two MASSES conspiracy trials, as well as the histories of the SEVEN ARTS and Arthur Moss's Village periodical QUILL. Margaret Anderson and Jane Heap's move to New York and their struggle to support the LITTLE REVIEW, including their trial for publishing James Joyce's ULYSSES, are covered in Chapter VII, "Three From Chicago." BROOM and SECESSION are briefly discussed in Chapter XI, "The Aesthetes."

Cleaton, Irene, and Allen Cleaton. BOOKS & BATTLES: AMERICAN LITERATURE, 1920-1930. New York: Cooper Square Publishers, 1970.

Chapter VII, "Payment in Fame," discusses the important literary periodicals of the 1920's. The REVIEWER, POETRY, the CHICAGO LITERARY TIMES, the AMERICAN MERCURY, and the BOOKMAN are viewed in detail.

Corrigan, Robert A. "Ezra Pound and the Bollingen Prize." MIDCONTINENT AMERICAN STUDIES JOURNAL, 8 (Fall 1967), 43-57.

In discussing the controversy over Pound's 1949 Bollingen Prize, Corrigan focuses on the clash between the SATURDAY REVIEW OF LITERATURE, which condemned the decision, and POETRY, which defended it.

Craven, Robert Kenton. "Seward Collins and the Traditionalists: A Study of the BOOKMAN and the AMERICAN REVIEW, 1928-1937." Dissertation, University of Kansas, 1967.

Collins edited the BOOKMAN from 1928 to 1933, and then the AMERICAN REVIEW from 1933 to 1937. Craven focuses on the traditionalist editorial outlook, and especially the view of the function of literature, that Collins brought to these periodicals.

Cray, Homer. "What Happens to a Manuscript after the Postman." BOOKMAN, 33 (1911), 653-55.

Although would-be contributors seldom believe it, periodical editors give all manuscripts a fair consideration in their search for high-quality material.

D., H.S. "Foreign Reviews: American Periodicals." CRITERION, 11 (1932), 361-63.

This article criticizes HARPER'S, the AMERICAN MERCURY, and the THINKER: "--all foster and feed on this strange snobism; never, of course, raise any real problem or to give any important information, but aimlessly titillate faculties which might, and should be usefully employed." The writer also criticizes Dudley Fitts in HOUND & HORN, who he feels is "inclined too little to running with the Hound, too much to hunting with the Horn; a great hullabaloo, but not a hare caught."

______. "Foreign Reviews: American Periodicals." CRITERION, 12 (1933), 540-44.

The writer notes that the main characteristic of current literary journals is "the increase of concern with Marxism and un-Marxism." He then analyzes the views on this issue found in SYMPOSIUM and HOUND & HORN, and discovers that "there are the same confusions, equivocations, and about the same amount of understanding which we would find anywhere." He concludes by attacking V.F. Calverton of the MODERN MONTHLY as a "social fascist."

Davenport, Walter, and James C. Derieux. LADIES, GENTLEMEN AND EDITORS. Garden City, N.Y.: Doubleday, 1960.

"A Ham, an Honest Rummy and a Hard Hater" (pp. 125-52) discusses the personalities and publications of Elbert Hubbard of the PHILISTINE, William Marion Reedy of REEDY'S MIRROR, and William Cowper Brann of the ICONOCLAST. Other journalistic figures viewed in this study include Sarah Josepha Hale, Joseph Dennie, and Benjamin Orange Flower.

Dell, Floyd. HOMECOMING: AN AUTOBIOGRAPHY. New York: Farrar & Rinehart, 1933.

Chapters XIX through XXIII cover Dell's activities in Chicago while he was editor of the FRIDAY LITERARY REVIEW, and chapters XXIV through XXXI cover the period during which he helped to edit the MASSES and the LIBERATOR in New York.

"Deserters from Fiction." NATION, 2 June 1910, p. 552.

The quantity and quality of periodical fiction have declined in the last five years, primarily because "the special article which has turned our newer and more popular magazines into gory battlefields of humanity has naturally served to crowd out the more idle teller of tales."

Deubach, Vila A. "A Survey of Social Conscience Short Stories in American Magazines, 1830-1930." Dissertation, University of Colorado, 1949.

DeVinne, Theodore L. "About Magazine Printing." LITERARY COLLECTOR, 4 (May-June 1902), 43-44.

DeVinne was printer of the CENTURY.

Drewry, John E. "American Magazines Today." SEWANEE REVIEW, 36 (1928), 342-56.

This article is a superficial examination of contemporary magazines, some of them literary.

_____. SOME MAGAZINES AND MAGAZINE MAKERS. Boston: Stratford Co., 1924.

This elementary study of American magazines includes individual sections on the following publications: The NORTH AMERICAN REVIEW (pp. 26-29), the AMERICAN MERCURY (pp. 44-48), the ATLANTIC (pp. 49-61), the CENTURY (pp. 61-64), SCRIBNER'S MAGAZINE (pp. 72-74), the COSMOPOLITAN MAGAZINE (pp. 101-4), LIFE (pp. 104-9), VANITY FAIR (pp. 109-11), and HARPER'S (pp. 112-13). These discussions are brief, general, and often include lengthy quotations from other secondary sources.

"Editing for the Best Magazines." ATLANTIC, 97 (1906), 719-20.

An anonymous editor admits that the rejection slip is "a survival of barbarism," but declares that, given the number of contributions sent to a periodical, personal notes are an impossibility. He is replying to the author of "On Writing for the Best Magazines," ATLANTIC, 97 (1906), 571-72.

Emmart, A.D. [Richel North]. "The Limitations of American Magazines." MODERN QUARTERLY, 1 (March 1923), 2-12; (July 1923), 18-30; (December 1923), 17-26.

Faxon, Frederick W. "Magazine Deterioration." BULLETIN OF BIBLIOGRAPHY, 9 (1916), 34-35.

Faxon introduces a list of popular magazines with the complaint that "an ever-increasing mass of trashy and oftentimes debasing 'literature' has appeared in new magazines." He fears a spread of this trend, because "COSMOPOLITAN, HEARST'S, McCLURE'S, have been won over already, CENTURY is weakening."

Foley, Richard Nicholas. "The Critical Reputation of Henry James in American Magazines from 1866 to 1916." Dissertation, Catholic University of America, 1944.

"Foreign Reviews: American Periodicals." CRITERION, 9 (1930), 369-73.

This article reviews the contents and policies of HARPER'S, the GYROSCOPE, and HOUND & HORN. HARPER'S is characterized as "middle-aged, conscious of bearing the burden in the heat of the day, and has neither the unwise liberty of youth nor the wise detachment of old age." The discussion of HOUND & HORN begins by calling it "the best magazine from the literary and philosophic-literary point of view of any in America."

Gillespie, Harris. "Magazine Mortality." MAGAZINE WORLD, 1 (October 1945), 27-30.

Gillespie explores the reasons for the high mortality rate for magazines throughout American history. He focuses on the CENTURY and the YOUTH'S COMPANION for discussion.

Hamburger, Philip. "Hardy Centennials." HARPER'S, 201 (October 1950), 37-40.

Hamburger presents "an imaginary glance at the manner in which several periodicals might conceivably celebrate their hundredth birthday, if they were old enough." His satire includes the NEW YORKER and PARTISAN REVIEW.

Hardwick, Elizabeth. "The Decline of Book Reviewing." HARPER'S, 219 (October 1959), 138-43.

The writer attacks the bland, superficial reviews found in the NEW YORK TIMES BOOK REVIEW, the SATURDAY REVIEW, and the HERALD TRIBUNE BOOK REVIEW.

Hausdorff, Don Mark. "Depression Laughter: Magazine Humor and American Society: 1929-1933." Dissertation, University of Minnesota, 1963.

______. "Magazine Humor and the Depression Years." NEW YORK FOLKLORE QUARTERLY, 20 (1964), 199-214.

Hausdorff examines the humor in the old LIFE, the NEW YORKER, the NEW MASSES, JUDGE, COLLEGE HUMOR, ESQUIRE, BALLYHOO, and AMERICANA. He concludes, "The irresponsibility and flippancy that had marked so much of the humor of the late 1920's was either disappearing or simply seemed anachronistic by the end of 1933." LIFE, JUDGE, and COLLEGE HUMOR suffered from this change, while the NEW YORKER and ESQUIRE adapted.

Hawthorne, Julian. "Journalism the Destroyer of Literature." CRITIC, 48 (1906), 166-71.

Journalistic concerns, including advertising, circulation, and illustration, have caused the exclusion from American periodicals of good literature chosen for its own sake.

Hicks, Granville. "'Sewanee,' 'Partisan,' 'Kenyon' and 'Hudson' Reviews: A Brief Analysis." NEW LEADER, 9 December 1957, pp. 9-10.

After examining the Fall 1957 issue of each review, Hicks concludes that they are much too cautious and conservative. The little magazines of the 1920's and 1930's were more courageous: "They were often enough wrongheaded in their rebelliousness, but at least the editors and contributors saw literature as a going concern and were on the side of the creators."

[Howells, William Dean]. "Editor's Easy Chair." HARPER'S, 114 (1907), 641-44.

Two fictional poets discuss the general quality of poetry published in periodicals.

"Is Genius Neglected by the Magazines?" CURRENT LITERATURE, 42 (1907), 165-66.

Contributors and would-be contributors offer differing opinions.

Janssens, G.A.M. THE AMERICAN LITERARY REVIEW: A CRITICAL HISTORY 1920-1950. The Hague: Mouton, 1968.

This detailed study includes chapters on the DIAL, HOUND & HORN, SYMPOSIUM, and the SOUTHERN REVIEW. Chapter VI, "The Forties and After," covers periodicals such as the KENYON REVIEW and PARTISAN REVIEW. The publishing histories and the literary personalities associated with these publications are thoroughly examined.

"A Jar for the Publisher." LITERARY DIGEST, 20 June 1914, pp. 1487-88.

An anonymous writer argues that he can make much more money by publishing his work in magazines than he can by selling to the book publishers. He feels that the young writer is better off if "he consistently ignores the book part of it and cultivates a magazine clientele."

Kazin, Alfred. "Writing for Magazines." CONTEMPORARIES. Boston: Little, Brown, 1962, pp. 469-74.

> Kazin feels that Anton Chekhov's light, casual approach to magazine writing could serve as a lesson to overly-serious magazinists: "A magazine is always a date, 'an issue,' a moment; it is created out of an exacting sense of time and it is about time. The spirit of the occasion, the tone of conversation, the modesty of the passing moment, are what most belong to it."

Kolars, Mary. "Some Modern Periodicals." CATHOLIC WORLD, 116 (1923), 781-89.

> After presenting a disparaging view of the American reading public, Kolars briefly evaluates the DIAL, the SMART SET, the NATION, the NEW REPUBLIC, and the FREEMAN.

Lanning, Brother Stephen Anthony. "Criticism in American Periodicals of the Prose Fiction of Booth Tarkington from 1899 to 1969." Dissertation, Catholic University of America, 1972.

> The fluctuations in the critical reception of Tarkington's work reflect the changes in literary taste of the periodicals.

"The Limbo of the Magazines." FREEMAN, 28 July 1920, pp. 461-63.

> This article attacks traditional American literature and criticism, and consequently the established magazines in which they appear.

Loftus, Beverly J.G. "Ezra Pound and the Bollingen Prize: The Controversy in Periodicals." JOURNALISM QUARTERLY, 39 (1962), 347-54, 394.

> Loftus examines articles and editorials on the controversy over Ezra Pound which appeared in twenty periodicals from 1949 to 1951, focusing on the SATURDAY REVIEW OF LITERATURE and POETRY, the first against the award and the last for it.

Lovett, Robert Morss. ALL OUR YEARS. New York: Viking Press, 1948.

> Lovett edited the DIAL under Martyn Johnson in 1919, immediately after the periodical moved to New York; he relates his experiences on pages 151-56. Chapter XI, "The 'New Republic,' 1921-1929," covers Lovett's association with that journal, including his work as book review editor. His discussion of both periodicals focuses on political issues. Nicholas Joost considers the DIAL section to be somewhat untrustworthy (see Nicholas Joost, "Culture vs. Power: Randolph Bourne, John Dewey, and THE DIAL," MIDWEST QUARTERLY, 9 [1968], 245-59).

Lyon, Mary. "The College Magazine . . . and After." MADEMOISELLE,

29 (August 1949), 250-51, 340-46.

This article discusses generally the problems facing the editors of college literary magazines, among them the competition from little magazines, previously independent, which had moved to campuses and become university- or college-sponsored. Short histories of the HARVARD ADVOCATE and the little magazine movement are included in this discussion.

"The Magazine from the Inside." BOOKMAN, 41 (1915), 251-60.

An anonymous magazine editor reveals many of the problems he faces which are not known to the public or to contributors.

"The Magazine in America." DOUBLE DEALER, 1 (1921), 82-83.

The writer finds one general fault with all periodicals publishing literary material in America, from the CENTURY and the ATLANTIC to the LITTLE REVIEW and the SMART SET: "These magazines can find any number of excuses for refusing a good thing and any number of excellent reasons (moral or financial) for accepting a bad one." A statement of the DOUBLE DEALER's intention to avoid this fault concludes the editorial.

Makosky, Donald Robin. "The Portrayal of Women in Wide-Circulation Magazine Short Stories, 1905-1955." Dissertation, University of Pennsylvania, 1966.

Makosky examines the portrayal of women and related issues of employment, courtship, and marriage as found in fiction from the following periodicals: WOMAN'S HOME COMPANION, COSMOPOLITAN, SATURDAY EVENING POST, HARPER'S, the SMART SET, and the NEW YORKER.

"The Manuscript Reader." ATLANTIC, 101 (1908), 863-64.

A magazine manuscript reader, remaining anonymous, tells of the difficulties of rejecting contributions from aspiring authors.

Marovitz, Sanford E. "Romance or Realism? Western Periodical Literature: 1893-1902." WESTERN AMERICAN LITERATURE, 10 (1975), 45-58.

Marovitz examines the Western fiction found in HARPER'S, the OVERLAND MONTHLY, COSMOPOLITAN, and McCLURE'S. He discovers that most of the material was unrealistic and sentimentalized.

May, Henry F. THE END OF AMERICAN INNOCENCE: A STUDY OF THE FIRST YEARS OF OUR OWN TIME, 1912-1917. New York: Alfred A. Knopf, 1959.

May examines the transition period that led American culture from nineteenth-century gentility to the modern era. He refers frequently to the magazines of the period, many of them literary. The NEW REPUBLIC, the MASSES, and the SEVEN ARTS are discussed individually on pages 314-28.

Mencken, H[enry] L[ouis]. "Memoirs of an Editor." VANITY FAIR, 41 (February 1934), 16, 54.

Mencken discusses the problems of editing a periodical, including the promises of manuscripts by professional writers. An editor "orders them all--but he receives only ten in every five hundred, and of the ten only one is fit to print."

Mott, Frank Luther. "College Literary Magazines." PALIMPSEST, 44 (1963), 303-10.

Mott briefly surveys the Iowa college literary magazines published in the late nineteenth and twentieth centuries, the most distinguished being AMERICAN PREFACES, which appeared from 1935 to 1943 at the University of Iowa.

_____. A HISTORY OF AMERICAN MAGAZINES. 5 vols. Cambridge, Mass.: Harvard University Press, 1957, 1968.

This is the most thorough study in the history of American magazines. Mott includes information on the history and economics of magazine publishing in general, and also studies of the editorial and publishing histories of individual periodicals. The following twentieth-century literary journals are examined individually in separate chapters. Volume II (1850-65): The NORTH AMERICAN REVIEW, the YOUTH'S COMPANION, HARPER'S, ATLANTIC. Volume III (1865-85): The OVERLAND MONTHLY, SCRIBNER'S-CENTURY, ST. NICHOLAS, PUCK, the DIAL (of Chicago and New York), JUDGE. Volume IV (1885-1905): The ARENA, the ARGOSY, the BIBELOT, the BLACK CAT, the BOOKMAN, COSMOPOLITAN, LIFE, the PHILISTINE, REEDY'S MIRROR, SCRIBNER'S MAGAZINE, the SEWANEE REVIEW. Volume V (1905-30): The AMERICAN MERCURY, the FREEMAN, the FUGITIVE, the LITTLE REVIEW, the MIDLAND, POETRY, the SMART SET, the SOUTH ATLANTIC QUARTERLY, the YALE REVIEW.

Mowery, M.B. "Convention of Themes in the Magazine Short Story." TEXAS REVIEW, 8 (1923), 369-83.

Magazine fiction is often written according to formula.

Muller, Herbert J. "The Function of a Critical Review." ARIZONA QUARTERLY, 4 (1948), 5-20.

The writer desires a nonspecialized, nonpartisan review that would publish, according to Matthew Arnold's view of literature and culture, the best that is known and thought in the world.

Munson, Gorham B. "Magazine Rack of the Washington Square Book Shop." STUDIES IN THE TWENTIETH CENTURY, no. 4 (Fall 1969), pp. 1-46.

Munson examines the editorial policies and histories of the following publications, all of which he eagerly read in the early 1920's: the NEW REPUBLIC, the NATION, the FREEMAN, the DIAL, the LITTLE REVIEW, VANITY FAIR, the MODERN SCHOOL, and the PLOWSHARE, the last published by Hervey White in Woodstock, New York, from 1912 to 1920 (first entitled the WILD HAWK). Munson contributed to some of these periodicals and was acquainted with their editors.

"Mushroom Reputations." BOOKMAN, 41 (1915), 402-4.

An editor complains that periodicals have become so concerned with publishing well-known writers that they sign long-range contracts and overpay for inferior material. This development, he claims, has led to a deterioration of the delicate relationship between editors and contributors.

Nathan, George Jean. "The Magazine in the Making." BOOKMAN, 34 (1911), 414-16.

More and more periodicals rely on regular staff writers, even for fiction, instead of depending on haphazard contributions.

______. "'Twice-Told Tales' of the Magazines." BOOKMAN, 34 (1912), 481-84.

To counteract the increasing occurrence of plagiarism, editors turned to a "reference" system, in which a contributor must either vouch for his work's originality or supply references from reputable people in the literary community.

______. "Why Manuscripts Are Rejected." BOOKMAN, 34 (1911), 143-47.

Nathan argues that editors, often criticized unfairly by would-be contributors, have valid reasons for rejecting manuscripts, reasons which may not be discernible to one unfamiliar with the periodical-publishing business.

"Of Editors and Their Critics." NORTH AMERICAN REVIEW, 183 (1906), 696-98.

This brief article defends periodical editors against charges of unfairness to would-be contributors.

"On Magazines and Manuscripts." BOOKMAN, 17 (1903), 3-4.

Prospective magazine contributors are advised that personal favoritism is never in the interest of an editor, and therefore is a negligible factor when decisions of acceptance or rejection are made.

Parker, Clara M. "The New Poetry and the Conservative American Magazine." TEXAS REVIEW, 6 (1920), 44-66.

Established periodicals are not receptive to unorthodox modern poetry.

Parry, Albert. GARRETS AND PRETENDERS: A HISTORY OF BOHEMIANISM IN AMERICA. New York: Dover, 1960.

Chapters XXIII and XXIV, "Fat Lasses for the MASSES" and "As to the Greatness of Their Art," cover the history of the MASSES and its relationship to Greenwich Village intellectual life. This is one of the studies attacked by Max Eastman in "Bunk about Bohemia," MODERN MONTHLY, 8 (1934), 200-208. Chapter XXVII, "Pound's Era," discusses a number of periodicals and their editors and contributors, including BROOM and SECESSION.

Perry, Bliss. "Literary Criticism in American Periodicals." THE PRAISE OF FOLLY AND OTHER PAPERS. Port Washington, N.Y.: Kennikat Press, 1964, pp. 171-231. First published in YALE REVIEW, NS 3 (1914), 635-55.

Perry criticizes the quality of book reviews and literary criticism in American periodicals. He blames the problem on the lack of a critical standard, commercialism, and public apathy.

Peterson, Theodore. MAGAZINES IN THE TWENTIETH CENTURY. 2nd ed. Urbana: University of Illinois Press, 1964.

This book covers the magazine field in general, and provides useful information on the economics of publishing, including advertising and the readership market. Chapter VI, "The Old Leaders that Died," views the passing of the NORTH AMERICAN REVIEW, SCRIBNER'S, the CENTURY, PUCK, LIFE, and JUDGE, among others, and presents the history of each publication. Chapter VIII, "New Leaders: The Missionaries," discusses the NEW YORKER and others. Chapter XIII, "Magazines for Cultural Minorities," does the same for the MASSES and the AMERICAN MERCURY.

______. "The Role of the Minority Magazine." ANTIOCH REVIEW, 23 (1963), 57-72.

Peterson examines the problems, most of them economic, faced by "magazines aimed at cultural minorities," and in the course of his discussion presents interesting statistics on circulation and budgets.

Read, Herbert. "Foreign Reviews: American Periodicals." MONTHLY CRITERION, 5 (1927), 165-72.

Read comments upon the contents and general quality of the following periodicals: the YALE REVIEW, the MODERN QUARTERLY, the DIAL, the AMERICAN MERCURY, HARPER'S, and the CENTURY.

_____. "Foreign Reviews: American Periodicals." MONTHLY CRITERION, 5 (1927), 369-74.

Read discusses the contents of current issues of the following periodicals: the YALE REVIEW, the NORTH AMERICAN REVIEW, the MODERN QUARTERLY, the DIAL, and the AMERICAN MERCURY. He comments on specific items as well as general literary quality.

"Serials versus Novels." DIAL, 57 (1914), 125-27.

American novels are inferior to English novels partly because American authors write serials for periodicals, and the limitations of this form hinder the artist's discursive freedom: "No pattern ever chosen by an artist in fiction is as elaborate as that to which the serial is pressed to adjust itself."

Soule, George. "Magazines and Democrats." NEW REPUBLIC, 21 August 1915, pp. 78-79.

Soule concludes that people who lament the quality of mass magazine fiction and blame the editors or book reviewers for bad public taste miss an essential truth: "Stories may be conventionalized and flat because of the application of a formula, but the formula exists not alone in the demand of the editors, but in the lives and tastes of the people, and doubtless also in the minds of most writers."

Stolberg, Benjamin. "Liberal Journalism: A House Divided." VANITY FAIR, 41 (September 1933), 22-23, 58.

Stolberg focuses on the NEW REPUBLIC and the NATION, and he concludes that their influence has been significant: "No doubt the new HARPER'S and SCRIBNER'S, the literary sections of our great dailies, our best periodical literature in general are nowadays less afraid of being 'highbrow' because of them."

Terwilliger, W. Bird. "A History of Literary Periodicals in Baltimore." Dissertation, University of Maryland, 1941.

Test, George A. "Francis Hackett: Literary Radical without Portfolio." MID-CONTINENT AMERICAN STUDIES JOURNAL, 5 (Fall 1964), 24-37.

Hackett founded and edited the "Friday Literary Review" of the CHICAGO EVENING POST from 1909 to 1911, and then served as literary editor of the NEW REPUBLIC from 1914 to 1922. Test examines the literary views, independent and often radical, expressed by Hackett in these periodicals.

Towne, Charles Hanson. ADVENTURES IN EDITING. New York: D. Appleton, 1926.

Towne held a number of editorial positions during his career. He began as an assistant to John Brisben Walker on COSMOPOLITAN, and then worked on the SMART SET, becoming its chief editor from 1904 to 1907. Subsequently, he did editorial work for the DELINEATOR, the DESIGNER, and McCLURE'S. This book reveals much about the day-to-day problems encountered by a literary editor.

Untermeyer, Louis. FROM ANOTHER WORLD: THE AUTOBIOGRAPHY OF LOUIS UNTERMEYER. New York: Harcourt, Brace, 1939.

In chapters entitled "Each Age Is a Dream" (pp. 37-63) and "World-Losers and World-Forsakers" (pp. 64-79), the poet discusses his work on the MASSES, as well as the two trials for conspiracy which he underwent with the periodical's editors during World War I. "Roots and Skyscrapers" (pp. 80-98) covers Untermeyer's association with James Oppenheim and the SEVEN ARTS. Also, in "The Bad Boy of Baltimore" (pp. 184-205) he views Mencken, primarily in relation to the AMERICAN MERCURY. Included is a letter from Mencken to the author describing his object in founding the journal.

Watkins, Ann. "Literature for Sale: The Agent Speaks." ATLANTIC, 168 (1941), 557-66.

A literary agent discusses the selling of literature to periodical editors and publishers.

Whittemore, Reed. LITTLE MAGAZINES. Pamphlets on American Writers, no. 32. Minneapolis: University of Minnesota Press, 1963.

Whittemore discusses the publishing history and editorial purpose of a number of periodicals, including POETRY, PARTISAN REVIEW, and the SOUTHERN REVIEW.

"Why Are Manuscripts Rejected? A Symposium." BOOKMAN, 43 (1916), 262-86.

The following editors are among those stating the policies of their periodicals: Robert Rudd Whiting of AINSLEE'S MAGAZINE, Ellery Sedgwick of the ATLANTIC, Douglas Doty of the CENTURY, Edgar Sisson of COSMOPOLITAN, George Jean Nathan of the SMART SET, and Frank Crowninshield of VANITY FAIR. An unsigned statement from HARPER'S is also included. The Nathan piece appeared as "Litany for Magazine Editors" in the SMART SET for February 1915, and also under H.L. Mencken's name in his BOOK OF BURLESQUES (New York: Knopf, 1924).

Wood, James Playsted. MAGAZINES IN THE UNITED STATES. 3rd ed. New York: Ronald Press, 1971.

This history deals with various kinds of magazines throughout American history. However, modern literary journals are discussed in chapter XVIII, "Magazine Satire and Humor: THE NEW YORKER," and chapter XXIV, "Some Changes in the National Magazine; The 'Little Magazines.'"

Zabel, Morton D[auwen]. "Recent Magazines." POETRY, 39 (1932), 345-49.

Among the periodicals reviewed are the SATURDAY REVIEW OF LITERATURE, HOUND & HORN, SYMPOSIUM, and HARPER'S. Of the last, Zabel concludes, "It is for the progressive editorial ineptitude . . . that it will finally be swept into a well-merited oblivion," citing an article in the periodical by Max Eastman as an example.

______. "Recent Magazines." POETRY, 45 (1934), 170-76.

Zabel laments the loss of good literary journals in the recent past, and then praises the SATURDAY REVIEW OF LITERATURE as the best literary weekly and the NEW REPUBLIC for returning to an interest in contemporary poetry, an interest it had held from 1914 to 1931 when Ridgely Torrence was its poetry editor.

______. "Recent Magazines." POETRY, 48 (1936), 51-56.

Zabel praises the new SOUTHERN REVIEW as a much-needed replacement for the loss earlier of the DIAL, the SYMPOSIUM, and HOUND & HORN. He then discusses the periodical's contents. He also mentions the bimonthly MAGAZINE: A JOURNAL OF CONTEMPORARY WRITING, which ended its three-year career in San Francisco the previous summer.

# Chapter 3

# GENERAL LITERARY PERIODICALS OF LARGE CIRCULATION

## GENERAL STUDIES

[Alden, Henry Mills]. "Editor's Study." HARPER'S, 129 (1914), 476-78.

HARPER'S and similar periodicals, including the ATLANTIC, have become less purely literary in response to the changing taste of the American reading public.

______. "Magazine Writing and Literature." NORTH AMERICAN REVIEW, 179 (1904), 341-56.

The editor of HARPER'S extolls the value of general nonspecialist periodicals such as his own and discusses their relationship to current literature. This essay appeared also in Alden's MAGAZINE WRITING AND THE NEW LITERATURE (New York: Harper and Brothers, 1908).

Allen, Frederick Lewis; William L. Chenery; and Fulton Oursler. "American Magazines, 1741-1941." BULLETIN OF THE NEW YORK PUBLIC LIBRARY, 45 (1941), 439-60.

Allen's essay is the only one pertinent to this bibliography. He traces the adjustments made by HARPER'S to the rise of the "cheap" magazines at the turn of the century, and the general changes which have occurred in the periodical's contents as a result of the Great Depression and then the outbreak of World War II. He also mentions the adjustments made by the ATLANTIC, the CENTURY, and SCRIBNER'S.

Bakeless, John. "Aristocrats of Publishing." VANITY FAIR, 40 (August 1933), 42-44, 52.

Bakeless points out the difficulties of the quality literary journals, such as HARPER'S and the ATLANTIC, in competing with the prosperous mass-circulation magazines.

Bode, Carl. MENCKEN. Carbondale: Southern Illinois University Press, 1969.

Chapter V, "The SMART SET Era," covers Mencken's coeditorship of that periodical from 1914 to 1923, and chapters XI and XII, "The MERCURY: The Web" and "The MERCURY: Mencken's Mind and Art," cover his personal relationships and editorial policies while running the second publication.

Bowles, J.M. "The Decorative Features of American Magazines: A Record and Review." PRINTING ART, 10 (1907), 241-47.

Bowles reviews the decorative art work, not illustrations, published in HARPER'S, SCRIBNER'S, and the CENTURY from 1901 to 1907. He names the specific artists and works which he feels are of permanent value.

Brown, Dorothy M. "The Quality Magazines in the Progressive Era." MID-AMERICA, 53 (1971), 139-59.

"A study of the qualities [sic] quest for survival, their aims and the thrust and pattern of their articles and editorials, not only redresses the staid image of ineffectual respectability but indicates that these magazines raised clear warning of the deep malaise of America." HARPER'S, the ATLANTIC, the CENTURY, and SCRIBNER'S are examined in detail.

Calkins, Earnest Elmo. "Magazine into Marketplace." SCRIBNER'S MAGAZINE, 1 (January 1937), 108-17.

Calkins traces the development of magazine advertising through the late nineteenth and early twentieth century, focusing on three quality periodicals, HARPER'S, SCRIBNER'S MONTHLY, and SCRIBNER'S MAGAZINE.

Chew, Samuel C., ed. FRUIT AMONG THE LEAVES: AN ANNIVERSARY ANTHOLOGY. New York: Appleton-Century-Crofts, 1950.

In an extensive introduction Chew relates in detail the histories of the CENTURY (founded as SCRIBNER'S MONTHLY) and ST. NICHOLAS, examining the various types of literature which appeared in them until their sale by the Century Company to other firms in 1930.

Drucker, Darrell I., Jr. "The Genteel Rebellion: A Study of American Journalistic Impressionism in Terms of Its Audience, 1880 to 1920." Dissertation, University of Minnesota, 1956.

Drucker examines TOWN TOPICS, M'LLE NEW YORK, the CRITERION, and the SMART SET, which he feels were created especially for the new industrial middle class which arose during the last quarter of the nineteenth century.

Gallishaw, John. "What the Quality Group Monthlies Are Buying." WRITER, 45 (1933), 97-101.

Gallishaw first discusses the characteristics which distinguish the fiction in HARPER'S, the ATLANTIC, and SCRIBNER'S from that published in the mass-circulation periodicals; he then differentiates the characteristics of the fiction found in each of the three.

Goldberg, Isaac. THE MAN MENCKEN: A BIOGRAPHICAL AND CRITICAL SURVEY. New York: Simon & Schuster, 1925.

Chapter VII (pp. 187-224) covers Mencken's work on the SMART SET and then the AMERICAN MERCURY.

Johnson, Burges. AS MUCH AS I DARE: A PERSONAL RECOLLECTION. New York: Ives Washington, 1944.

In chapter VIII, "Franklin Square," Johnson relates his experiences as a staff member of HARPER'S and an employee of Harper and Brothers. Among his activities discussed in chapter IX, "A Rolling Stone," is his editorship of JUDGE.

Kemler, Edgar. THE IRREVERENT MR. MENCKEN. Boston: Little, Brown, 1950.

Chapter V (pp. 55-69) of this biography presents information on Mencken's editorship, along with George Jean Nathan of the SMART SET, and chapters XI through XIV (pp. 155-234) his editorship of the AMERICAN MERCURY.

King, Alexander. "The Sad Case of the Humorous Magazines." VANITY FAIR, 41 (December 1933), 26-27, 68, 71.

King writes about the rise and fall of various humor magazines, including LIFE, JUDGE, and PUCK.

Manchester, William. DISTURBER OF THE PEACE: THE LIFE OF H.L. MENCKEN. New York: Harper and Brothers, 1951.

Some of Mencken's activities as SMART SET editor are related on pages 69-80, including his wooing of a female contributor in order to get more stories for the periodical. Pages 148-59 emphasize the strong hand he took in editing the AMERICAN MERCURY, thus leaving the stamp of his own personality on the publication.

Mayfield, Sara. THE CONSTANT CIRCLE: H.L. MENCKEN AND HIS FRIENDS. New York: Delacorte Press, 1968.

Chapter I, "Baltimore Days," includes information on Mencken's editorship of the SMART SET with George Jean Nathan. Chapter V, "Freelance Days," and following chapters contain information on Mencken and the AMERICAN MERCURY.

Mencken, H[enry] L[ouis]. LETTERS OF H.L. MENCKEN. Ed. Guy J. Forgue. New York: Alfred A. Knopf, 1961.

Many letters in this annotated and indexed collection reveal Mencken as editor of the SMART SET and the AMERICAN MERCURY. Among the most interesting letters is one to George Jean Nathan in which their growing rift during the MERCURY period is apparent (pp. 268-70).

Nathan, George Jean. "The Happiest Days of H.L. Mencken." ESQUIRE, 48 (October 1957), 146-50.

Nathan reminisces about the SMART SET and AMERICAN MERCURY days.

Oberfirst, Robert. "Analysis of a Quality Magazine Short Short Story." WRITER, 57 (1944), 77-81.

Oberfirst analyzes an ATLANTIC story by Ben Hur Lampman entitled "Blinker Was a Good Dog." He concludes that fiction published in the quality periodicals has as a primary element the "significance of theme" and that the "plot action is always subordinate to the characterization."

Peffer, Nathaniel. "Editors and Essays: A Note on Magazines Like HARPER'S." HARPER'S, 172 (1935), 78-84.

The "old-line" magazines, HARPER'S, SCRIBNER'S, and the ATLANTIC, have turned from their former exclusive interest in belles lettres, including familiar essays, to journalistic pieces on contemporary political and social problems. Peffer concludes that "the old-line magazines, American literature, and American culture are the better therefor."

Porter, William. "The Quality Magazines and the New American Reader." GAZETTE, 6 (1960), 305-10.

Porter notes that the importance of "quality" magazines has declined since the 1920's, and that the circulation of the ATLANTIC, HARPER'S, and the NEW YORKER is quite modest. He concludes that "the increasing fractionation and specialization of interest among well-educated Americans is the chief reason for anticipating only a declining future for the quality magazines."

Simpson, Herbert M. "Mencken and Nathan." Dissertation, University of Maryland, 1965.

Simpson studies the literary and journalistic accomplishments of

Mencken and Nathan while they were editors of the SMART SET and the AMERICAN MERCURY.

Stegner, Wallace. THE UNEASY CHAIR: A BIOGRAPHY OF BERNARD DE-VOTO. Garden City, N.Y.: Doubleday, 1974.

Pages 160-97 of this biography cover in detail DeVoto's editorship of the SATURDAY REVIEW OF LITERATURE from 1936 to 1938, a tenure that held more frustrations than rewards for him. DeVoto's relationship with HARPER'S, for which he wrote "The Editor's Easy Chair" column, and his early editorship of the HARVARD GRAD-UATE'S MAGAZINE are also examined.

Stenerson, Douglas C. H.L. MENCKEN: ICONOCLAST FROM BALTIMORE. Chicago: University of Chicago Press, 1971.

Focusing on Mencken's editorship of the SMART SET and his early years on the AMERICAN MERCURY, "this book examines and evaluates Mencken's part in precipitating and perpetuating the great quarrel within American culture which developed between his boyhood in the 1880s and 90s and his heyday in the 1920s."

Towne, Charles Hanson. SO FAR SO GOOD. New York: Julian Messner, 1945.

Chapter XII covers the author's experiences on COSMOPOLITAN (pp. 81-97). Also, chapters XIII and XIV cover the SMART SET (pp. 98-121), and chapter XVIII discusses editor Theodore Dreiser and the DELINEATOR (pp. 144-55). Some of this information, at times word for word, is found in his ADVENTURES IN EDITING.

Whipple, Leon. "The Revolution on Quality Street." SURVEY-GRAPHIC, 57 (1926-27), 119-24, 177-79, 427-32, 469-72.

Whipple examines the changes which the quality periodicals have undergone since the turn of the century. He discusses in detail the contents, format, policies, and circulation figures of the AT-LANTIC, the CENTURY, SCRIBNER'S, HARPER'S, and the FORUM. He also discusses the arrival of H.L. Mencken's AMERICAN MER-CURY. One of Whipple's main points is the abandonment of illustration by the very periodicals which pioneered in that field in the nineteenth century.

## STUDIES OF INDIVIDUAL PERIODICALS

### THE AMERICAN MERCURY (1924-current)

Angoff, Charles. "The Beginning Writer and THE AMERICAN MERCURY."

WRITER, 63 (1950), 253-55.

The managing editor of the MERCURY expresses an eagerness for the work of new, unknown writers. At times the editors even solicit work from aspiring unknowns.

______. "From Mencken . . . to Maguire: The Tragedy of the AMERICAN MERCURY." ADL BULLETIN, 14 (May 1957), 4-6.

Angoff describes the changes in the MERCURY's policies and content after Mencken's editorship.

______. H.L. MENCKEN: A PORTRAIT FROM MEMORY. New York: Thomas Yoseloff, 1956.

"My purpose is simply to describe Mencken--and, by corollary, his time--only as I saw and heard him, as his associate on the AMERICAN MERCURY and also as a personal friend." Angoff worked on the MERCURY under Mencken, was himself the editor from May 1934 to April 1935, and remained associated with the jour ɹl in later years.

______. "The Inside View of Mencken's MERCURY." NEW REPUBLIC, 13 September 1954, pp. 18-22.

Angoff assesses the strengths and weaknesses of Mencken's editorship. He concludes that Mencken "was a man of contradictions and absurdities, and puerilities and even cheapness, but he was a great editor, and his MERCURY was, all in all, a great magazine."

Christian, Henry A. "'What Else Have You in Mind?': Louis Adamic and H.L. Mencken." MENCKENIANA, 47 (Fall 1973), 1-12.

This article traces the relationship between Adamic, a contributor to the MERCURY, and Mencken.

Cousins, Norman. "Our Times and the MERCURY." SATURDAY REVIEW, 12 June 1954, p. 20.

Cousins describes the debunking spirit of the MERCURY and discusses the reasons for the journal's decline. One reason he offers: "To be totally without respect for the mechanism of hope in man as were the editors of the MERCURY was to live in the wrong century."

Drewry, John E. "The AMERICAN MERCURY--Still Reflecting Mencken's Molding Hand." CONTEMPORARY AMERICAN MAGAZINES: A SELECTED BIBLIOGRAPHY AND REPRINTS OF ARTICLES DEALING WITH VARIOUS PERIODICALS. 3rd ed. Athens: University of Georgia Press, 1938, pp. 5-9.

Drewry extensively quotes Mencken and later editors, especially Gordon Carroll, the current managing editor, on the MERCURY's policies.

Hays, Arthur Garfield. LET FREEDOM RING. New York: Horace Liveright, 1928.

In "Freedom of the Press" (pp. 155-92), Hays discusses his defense of Mencken and the MERCURY in the 1926 Boston Hatrack case. Hays considered the case part of a general struggle against the censorship which had caused periodicals, including the MASSES, to be driven out of business.

Kloefkorn, Johnny L. A CRITICAL STUDY OF THE WORK OF H.L. MENCKEN AS LITERARY EDITOR AND CRITIC OF THE AMERICAN MERCURY. The Emporia State Research Studies, vol. 7, no. 4. Emporia: Graduate Division of the Kansas State Teachers College, 1959.

Kloefkorn's thesis shows "Mencken's gradual indifference toward *belles lettres*, his increasing obstinacy in fields political, his surprising obtuseness and contradiction, his final desertion of the literary scene."

Manchester, William. "Mencken and the MERCURY." HARPER'S, 201 (August 1950), 65-73.

This article covers the founding of the MERCURY, Mencken's editorial policies, the immediate financial success of the periodical, and the extreme public reaction both for and against the views expressed in it.

Manglaviti, Leo M.J. "Faulkner's 'That Evening Sun' and Mencken's 'Best Editorial Judgment.'" AMERICAN LITERATURE, 43 (1972), 649-54.

Manglaviti examines the typescript of "That Evening Sun" and correspondence between Faulkner and Mencken. He reveals that Mencken requested a number of changes in the story for publication in the MERCURY, some to avoid offending the public.

Maynard, Theodore. "Mencken Leaves 'The American Mercury.'" CATHOLIC WORLD, 139 (1934), 10-20.

Maynard reviews Mencken's editorial policies, and states, "We may get a very good magazine from Mr. Hazlitt, but it is bound to be a different magazine under the old name."

Mott, Frank Luther. "THE AMERICAN MERCURY." MENCKENIANA, 22 (Summer 1967), 9-10.

This short history consists of prepublication excerpts from the final volume of Mott's A HISTORY OF AMERICAN MAGAZINES, cited in chapter 2.

O'Brien, Adrian Philip. "A Critical Study of the Editorials of Henry Louis

Mencken in the AMERICAN MERCURY from January 1924 to December 1933." Dissertation, St. John's University, 1959.

R[ead], H[erbert]. "Foreign Reviews: American Periodicals." CRITERION, 6 (1927), 571-76.

Included in this review is high praise for the MERCURY. Read states, "Of one thing I am convinced: it is an indigenous culture, and there is no parallel in England--no parallel and no possibility of a parallel. To appreciate and understand the AMERICAN MERCURY implies *a priori* interest in the American scene."

Salzman, Jack. "Conroy, Mencken, and THE AMERICAN MERCURY." JOURNAL OF POPULAR CULTURE, 7 (1973), 524-28.

Mencken corresponded with and published work by Jack Conroy from 1930 to 1933, refuting the general view that he was totally unsympathetic to leftists, and that the MERCURY had declined to a third-rate publication by then. At that time he also published work by such writers as William Faulkner, Erskine Caldwell, and James T. Farrell.

Simpson, Herbert M. "Dating a Mencken Letter." MENCKENIANA, 22 (Summer 1967), 5-7.

Simpson disputes Guy J. Forgue's dating of a letter from Mencken to George Jean Nathan (see H.L. Mencken, LETTERS OF H.L. MENCKEN, cited in the General Studies section of this chapter, above, pp. 249-50). Forgue, who edited Mencken's letters, dates it May 3, 1923, but Simpson argues: "He assumes that it deals with plans for the as yet untitled new magazine, the MERCURY. Actually it deals with plans for a change in editorial arrangement of the already established MERCURY." Therefore it must have been written in 1925.

Singleton, M.K. "History of the AMERICAN MERCURY under the Editorship of Henry Mencken, 1924 to 1933." Dissertation, Duke University, 1960.

______. H.L. MENCKEN AND THE *AMERICAN MERCURY* ADVENTURE. Durham, N.C.: Duke University Press, 1962.

Mencken's founding and editing of the MERCURY from 1924 to 1933 are examined in detail. Singleton also studies Mencken's relationships with writers, editors, and other public figures during this time. This study is closely based upon Singleton's dissertation, listed above.

Spivak, Lawrence E., and Charles Angoff, eds. THE *AMERICAN MERCURY* READER; A SELECTION OF DISTINGUISHED ARTICLES, STORIES, AND POEMS PUBLISHED IN *THE AMERICAN MERCURY* DURING THE PAST TWENTY YEARS.

Garden City, N.Y.: Blue Ribbon Books, 1946.

The foreword states that this anthology gives "an idea of the character and wide scope of the magazine" and explains "the influential and respected place it has won in American periodical journalism."

Sycherley, H. Alan. "Mencken and Knopf: The Editor and His Publisher." AMERICAN QUARTERLY, 16 (1964), 460-72.

This analysis of the friendship includes a study of the years when Mencken edited the MERCURY for Knopf. Although their views diverged in later years, their respect for each other remained constant.

THREE YEARS, 1924 TO 1927; THE STORY OF A NEW IDEA AND ITS SUCCESSFUL ADAPTATION. New York: American Mercury, 1927.

Only 600 copies of this forty-five-page pamphlet were printed, and each was signed by the editor and publisher. Mencken supplied a postscript.

See also studies by Bode, Goldberg, Kemler, Manchester, Mayfield, Nathan, Simpson, Stenerson, and Mencken's LETTERS, listed in the General Studies section of this chapter, above.

ATLANTIC MONTHLY (1857-current)

Allen, Frederick Lewis. "The American Magazine Grows Up." ATLANTIC, 180 (November 1947), 77-82.

The editor of the ATLANTIC sketches the history of his literary journal from the mid-nineteenth century to the present.

______. "Sedgwick and the ATLANTIC." OUTLOOK AND INDEPENDENT, 150 (1928), 1406-8, 1417.

Ellery Sedgwick bought the ATLANTIC in 1908 and edited it from 1909 to 1938. He is described as having saved the periodical by including more articles on current issues and events.

Drewry, John E. "The ATLANTIC MONTHLY--Learned But Readable." CONTEMPORARY AMERICAN MAGAZINES: A SELECTED BIBLIOGRAPHY AND REPRINTS OF ARTICLES DEALING WITH VARIOUS PERIODICALS. 3rd ed. Athens: University of Georgia Press, 1938, pp. 10-14.

In the course of his discussion of the ATLANTIC's policies under Ellery Sedgwick, Drewry extensively quotes from Frederick Lewis Allen's article in the OUTLOOK AND INDEPENDENT (cited above).

Gallup, Donald. "Gertrude Stein and the ATLANTIC." YALE UNIVERSITY LIBRARY GAZETTE, 28 (1954), 109-28.

This article includes the correspondence between Gertrude Stein and Ellery Sedgwick, ATLANTIC editor, written between 1919 and 1933. Sedgwick eventually published some of her writing.

Sedgwick, Ellery. THE HAPPY PROFESSION. Boston: Little, Brown, 1946.

Chapters XIII to XXIV, the last half of the book, cover Sedgwick's experiences while editor of the ATLANTIC.

_____, comp. ATLANTIC HARVEST: MEMOIRS OF THE ATLANTIC, WHEREIN ARE TO BE FOUND STORIES, ANECDOTES, AND OPINIONS, CONTROVERSIAL AND OTHERWISE, TOGETHER WITH A VARIETY OF MATTER, RELEVANT AND IRRELEVANT, ACCOMPANIED BY CERTAIN OBDURATE CONVICTIONS. Boston: Little, Brown, 1947.

Sedgwick's introductory essay, "To the Reader, Gentle and Ungentle" (pp. ix-xxxv), includes anecdotes relating to his editorship of the ATLANTIC.

Warren, Dale. "'Weeks'--of the ATLANTIC." PUBLISHER'S WEEKLY, 12 August 1939, pp. 448-51.

Warren reviews Edward Weeks's accomplishments while editor of the ATLANTIC, a position he assumed in July of 1938. One of the changes he brought about is that "the ATLANTIC appears today with more text than ever before in its history," including an extra thirty pages each issue for three serialized novels a year.

Weeks, Edward. MY GREEN AGE. Boston: Little, Brown, 1973.

Chapters VII to X (pp. 199-326) cover Weeks's work on the ATLANTIC and for the Atlantic Monthly Press, from 1924 until he became firmly established as the periodical's editor in 1939, when Richard and Barbara Danielson bought the publication from Ellery Sedgwick. Weeks reveals in detail his association with Sedgwick and the struggles faced by the ATLANTIC's staff during the Depression.

_____. "'We Have Read with Interest.'" ATLANTIC, 143 (1929), 735-44.

The ATLANTIC offices handle 40,000 literary contributions a year, and Weeks describes "some of the homemade products that are pouring into our magazine offices, and the thought that has gone into their making."

Weeks, Edward, and Emily Flint, eds. JUBILEE: ONE HUNDRED YEARS OF

THE ATLANTIC. Boston: Little, Brown, 1957.

Short introductions to each section of this anthology offer background information on the writers and policies of the periodical.

## THE BOOKMAN (1895-1933)

"THE BOOKMAN." HOUND & HORN, 1 (1927), 175-77.

This short article reviews the issues of September through November 1927, the first under Burton Rascoe's editorship. However, the improvements "are so few in number, and the proportion between them and the twaddle so overpoweringly great, that only the most wildly optimistic will see in them a cause to hope for better things to come."

Cook, George. "London's BOOKMAN Letters." JACK LONDON NEWSLETTER, 6 (May-August 1973), 81-87.

Doran, George H. CHRONICLES OF BARABBAS, 1884-1934. New York: Harcourt, Brace, 1935.

Doran tells of his experiences as a publisher, including those relating to his ten-year ownership of the BOOKMAN.

Maurice, Arthur Bartlett. "Old Bookman Days." BOOKMAN, 66 (1927), 20-26; "More 'Old Bookman Days.'" BOOKMAN, 70 (1929), 56-65.

Maurice was editor of the BOOKMAN from 1907 to 1917, succeeding Harry Thurston Peck. He reminisces about his relationship with Peck before 1907, and his association with prominent writers of the period. The first installment relates more specifically to his BOOKMAN experiences than does the second.

## THE CENTURY ILLUSTRATED MONTHLY MAGAZINE (1881-1929), originally called SCRIBNER'S MONTHLY (1870-81)

Albert, Dora. "A Veteran Editor Talks of Magazine Problems." WRITER, 42 (1930), 31-34.

Hewitt H. Howland, editor of the CENTURY since 1925, discusses his reasons for changing the periodical from a monthly to a quarterly. He also presents some of his general editorial views.

"The CENTURY Magazine 1870-1924." PAN-AMERICAN MAGAZINE, 37 (1924), 341-58.

This article sketches the periodical's history.

Drewry, John E. "The FORUM-CENTURY: Dedicated to Open-Mindedness." WRITER, 49 (1936), 20-21, 25-26.

Drewry discusses the editorial policies of the periodical, and then briefly traces the editorial histories of both the FORUM and CENTURY up to the absorption of the CENTURY by the FORUM in 1930.

Johnson, Robert Underwood. REMEMBERED YESTERDAYS. Boston: Little, Brown, 1923.

Johnson, editor of the CENTURY from 1909 to 1913 following the death of Richard Watson Gilder, discusses the work of the journal's various editors in chapter IV, "Forty Years of Editing: 1873-1913."

_____. "The Responsibilities of the Magazine." INDEPENDENT, 73 (1912), 1487-90.

The editor of the CENTURY considers "the responsibility, first, for accuracy; second, for impartiality; and, last of all, for tone." Tone "may be said to include style, taste and moral influence."

Larson, Lawrence H. THE PRESIDENT WORE SPATS: A BIOGRAPHY OF GLENN FRANK. Madison: State Historical Society of Wisconsin, 1965.

Chapter IV, "The CENTURY Magazine," covers Frank's associate editorship from 1919 to 1925, during which he changed the format and contents of the periodical in an attempt to make it more competitive with the new cheap magazines, an attempt only partially successful at best.

## COSMOPOLITAN MAGAZINE (1886-current), entitled HEARST'S INTERNATIONAL COMBINED WITH COSMOPOLITAN (1925-52)

Drewry, John E. "HEARST'S INTERNATIONAL-COSMOPOLITAN--All Star, But Hospitable to Newcomers." CONTEMPORARY AMERICAN MAGAZINES: A SELECTED BIBLIOGRAPHY AND REPRINTS OF ARTICLES DEALING WITH VARIOUS PERIODICALS. 3rd ed. Athens: University of Georgia Press, 1938, pp. 31-34.

Drewry sketches COSMOPOLITAN's editing and publishing history to its merger with HEARST'S INTERNATIONAL in 1925.

McIntyre, O.O. "Happy Birthday to You, COSMOPOLITAN." HEARST'S INTERNATIONAL-COSMOPOLITAN, 100 (April 1936), 17, 160-61.

McIntyre, who contributed to COSMOPOLITAN for fourteen years, relates some of the literary associations he developed through the periodical, and states, "Indeed, you may name your favorite author of the past fifty years and be almost assured he or she has appeared often within the pages of the magazine."

FRIDAY LITERARY REVIEW (1909-14)

Tanselle, G. Thomas. "Floyd Dell in the 'Friday Literary Review.'" PAPERS OF THE BIBLIOGRAPHICAL SOCIETY OF AMERICA, 57 (1963), 371-76.

Dell's contributions to the REVIEW are listed, including poems, essays, reviews, and editorials. He edited the publication from July 28, 1911, to September 26, 1913.

______. "The 'Friday Literary Review' and the Chicago Renaissance." JOURNALISM QUARTERLY, 38 (1961), 332-36.

Under the guidance of editor Francis Hackett, followed by Floyd Dell and then Lucian and Augusta Cary, this literary supplement to the CHICAGO EVENING POST became a leading review and a major contribution to the Chicago Renaissance from 1909 to 1914.

HARPER'S MONTHLY MAGAZINE (1850-current)

Alden, Henry Mills. "An Anniversary Retrospect: 1900-1910." HARPER'S, 121 (1910), 38-45.

The editor of HARPER'S reviews the changes in the periodical during the previous ten years, including an increase in the number of short stories and a decrease in serialized novels. He concludes that HARPER'S keeps abreast of new trends in literature and other fields.

[______]. "Editor's Study." HARPER'S, 104 (1902), 675-78.

Alden discusses the types of contribution he receives, and his concern for reader interest in the material he finally selects.

[______]. "Editor's Study." HARPER'S, 105 (1902), 484-86.

This piece reviews in general terms Alden's relationships with contributors, prospective contributors, and readers.

[______]. "Editor's Study." HARPER'S, 105 (1902), 646-48.

The editor states that his periodical has an "organic unity" dictated by the class and interests of his readers. He also says that certain types of articles, such as those on current affairs, or on highly technical subjects, are excluded because they are found in abundance in other publications.

[______]. "Editor's Study." HARPER'S, 106 (1902), 816-18.

Alden discusses the editorial policies of nonspecialist periodicals such as HARPER'S.

[______]. "Editor's Study." HARPER'S, 112 (1906), 638-40.

In reply to a reader's inquiry Alden points out that HARPER'S has dropped the serial publication of novels, and articles on current and historical events. As a result, short stories have become more prominent in the periodical.

[______]. "Editor's Study." HARPER'S, 117 (1908), 961-64.

The editorial policies of HARPER'S are discussed, especially the trend toward publication of scientific articles, which Alden says began in 1870.

Allen, Frederick L[ewis]. "HARPER'S MAGAZINE" 1850-1950: A CENTENARY ADDRESS. New York: Newcomen Society in North America, 1950.

In the second half of this address, Allen explains the significant changes made in format and editorial outlook by Thomas B. Wells, editor from 1919 to 1931. He closes by stating the current editorial aims and policies of HARPER'S. This piece first appeared as "One Hundred Years of HARPER'S," HARPER'S, 201 (October 1950), 23-36. It was revised for publication as a booklet.

Butterfield, L.H. "Bernard DeVoto in the Easy Chair: 1935-1955." NEW ENGLAND QUARTERLY, 29 (1956), 435-42.

Unhampered by editorial control, DeVoto freely discussed the strengths and weaknesses of American culture in "The Easy Chair" column in HARPER'S.

Canby, Henry Seidel. "HARPER'S MAGAZINE--A National Institution." HARPER'S, 151 (1925), 513-21.

Canby reviews the periodical's history, including the editorial policies and the contents after 1900. This article was published as a pamphlet, HARPER'S MAGAZINE--A NATIONAL INSTITUTION. New York: Harper and Brothers, 1925.

Collier, Sargent. "HARPER'S MAGAZINE and Its Editor: An Hour with Lee Hartman." WRITER, 46 (1934), 273-76.

Hartman, editor since 1931, generally discusses HARPER'S. This article reviews the modern history of the periodical, including its radical change in 1919 under Thomas Bucklin Wells from a family illustrated journal to a more vigorous and provocative publication.

DeVoto, Bernard. "The Constant Function." HARPER'S, 201 (October 1950), 215-20.

DeVoto maintains that HARPER'S is one of a few periodicals which perform a vital function for American society--to inform a serious and intellectual minority of new ideas ignored by magazines aimed at the general public.

______. THE EASY CHAIR. Boston: Houghton Mifflin, 1955.

In a preface to this collection DeVoto discusses the journalistic tone of "The Easy Chair," a column in HARPER'S, and briefly views the work of his predecessors (pp. vii-x). In a section entitled "Number 241 (November 1955)" he discusses the critical attitude he has developed in the column since he succeeded Edward S. Martin in 1935, and the reactions he has received from various segments of his reading public (pp. 3-11). "The Third Floor (March 1952)" replies to those who criticize his reformist ideas (pp. 31-38). He notes that his predecessors, especially George William Curtis and William Dean Howells, also called for needed reforms in their day.

Drewry, John E. "HARPER'S Magazine--Where Ideas Are Hatched." CONTEMPORARY AMERICAN MAGAZINES: A SELECTED BIBLIOGRAPHY AND REPRINTS OF ARTICLES DEALING WITH VARIOUS PERIODICALS. 3rd ed. Athens: University of Georgia Press, 1938, pp. 27-30.

This short sketch focuses on developments such as the 1925 modernization of contents and physical appearance of HARPER'S.

Exman, Eugene. THE HOUSE OF HARPER: ONE HUNDRED AND FIFTY YEARS OF PUBLISHING. New York: Harper & Row, 1967.

The periodical's modern history, including its successful struggle to adapt to changing public taste, is covered in chapter XXI, "HARPER'S MAGAZINE (1900-1967)."

Fischer, John, ed. SIX IN THE EASY CHAIR. Urbana: University of Illinois Press, 1973.

This is a collection of the editor's "Easy Chair" columns by the six men who have held the position: Donald Grant Mitchell, George William Curtis, William Dean Howells, Edward S. Martin, Bernard DeVoto, and Fischer himself. The introduction (pp. 1-10) and the biographical sketches provide information on the history of HARPER'S and the role these men have played in it.

Fischer, John, and Lucy Donaldson, eds. HUMOR FROM HARPER'S. New York: Harper and Brothers, 1961.

Fischer begins his brief survey in the introduction (pp. xii-xiv) by declaring that "some of the worst humor that ever reached print appeared in HARPER'S MAGAZINE." He concludes, however, that "the editors . . . have always tried, even in the genteel years of the nineteenth century, to publish humor that says something worth saying."

Hough, Robert L. THE QUIET REBEL: WILLIAM DEAN HOWELLS AS SOCIAL COMMENTATOR. Lincoln: University of Nebraska, 1959.

In chapter VI, "Howells and Reform: 1896-1920," Hough notes the following of the "Editor's Easy Chair" column, which Howells wrote from 1900-1920: "Undoubtedly the fact that he had to write 3,000 words each month for the magazine provided a stimulus to his thought, but it is clear that this thought continued primarily in a social direction."

Howells, William Dean. "Editor's Easy Chair." HARPER'S, 129 (1914), 476-78.

HARPER'S and other periodicals have become less purely literary because of changes in public taste.

______. "In Memoriam." HARPER'S, 140 (1919), 133-36.

Howells praises Alden and gives an inside, anecdotal view of Alden's long career as editor of HARPER'S.

______. W.D. HOWELLS AS CRITIC. Ed. Edwin H. Cady. Boston: Routledge & Kegan Paul, 1973.

"In and out of 'The Easy Chair,' 1901-20" (pp. 335-475), contains essays written for HARPER'S and the NORTH AMERICAN REVIEW. Cady prefaces this section with an account of Howell's acceptance of the position with HARPER'S and the critical attitude with which he took on the commitment.

Knowles, Horace, ed. GENTLEMEN, SCHOLARS AND SCOUNDRELS: A TREASURY OF THE BEST OF HARPER'S MAGAZINE FROM 1850 TO THE PRESENT. New York: Harper and Brothers, 1959.

This is the latest of numerous editions from 1915. John Fischer's introduction reviews the periodical's history, and the anthology itself presents a portrait of HARPER'S through the years.

Kouwenhoven, John A. "Personal & Otherwise." HARPER'S, 201 (October 1950), 8-20.

The writer traces changes in the editorial policies of HARPER'S, notably the emphasis since 1920 "less upon sight than insight, less upon appreciative sensibility than upon analytical understanding."

Lee, Robert Edson. "The Easy Chair Essays of Bernard DeVoto: A Finding List." BULLETIN OF BIBLIOGRAPHY AND MAGAZINE NOTES, 23 (1960), 64-69.

"It is the purpose of this finding list with its minimum of annotation to exhume the 243 Easy Chair essays by DeVoto."

LIFE (1883-1936)

Bridges, Robert. "The First Years." LIFE, 4 January 1923, p. 23.

Bridges, who wrote "Bookishness," a column of satirical reviews using the name Droch, discusses his work under founder and editor John Ames Mitchell.

Downey, Fairfax. PORTRAIT OF AN ERA, AS DRAWN BY C.D. GIBSON. New York: Charles Scribner's Sons, 1936.

Gibson was associated with LIFE from 1885; chapter IV, "LIFE and Hope," and chapters following, cover this association. Chapter XIX, "Artist into Editor," relates Gibson's disappointing and exhausting experiences as LIFE's editor from 1920 until 1932, when he sold the periodical to Clair Maxwell and Henry Richter.

Flautz, John. LIFE: THE GENTLE SATIRIST. Bowling Green, Ohio: Bowling Green University Popular Press, 1972.

This study focuses on the periodical's publishing and editing history up to 1918, when founder and editor John Ames Mitchell died. An appendix (pp. 189-93) relates the "Relevant Histories of PUCK and JUDGE," LIFE's main rivals.

Hagemann, E.R. "LIFE Buffets (and Comforts) Henry James, 1883-1916: An Introduction and an Annotated Checklist." PAPERS OF THE BIBLIOGRAPHICAL SOCIETY OF AMERICA, 62 (1968), 207-25.

"A year rarely passed that somewhere, somehow, LIFE did not confront James, and for good measure throw an occasional missile at his distinguished brother." Hagemann begins with a sketch of the periodical's history, and concludes with a lengthy "Annotated Check List of Jamesiana in LIFE" (pp. 211-25).

______. "Stephen Crane Faces the Storms of LIFE, 1896-1901." JOURNAL OF POPULAR CULTURE, 2 (1968), 347-60.

Hagemann examines the attitudes expressed toward Crane by LIFE's writers, ranging from positive reviews of his work to burlesques of his style, to an obituary that comments on his missed opportunities.

_____. "'Unexpected Light in Shady Places': Henry James and LIFE, 1883-1916." WESTERN HUMANITIES REVIEW, 24 (1970), 241-50.

LIFE "gibed, scoffed at, insulted, praised, and occasionally respected the style and work of Henry James, Jr., in a wondrous variety of ways on approximately 270 occasions."

"How Mitchell, of 'Life' Made Humor Do Things." PRINTER'S INK, 11 July 1918, pp. 39-40.

Mitchell's policies as editor are briefly discussed, including his tolerance of the diverse points of view of his writers and illustrators.

Martin, Edward S. Untitled article. LIFE, 4 January 1923, pp. 16-18.

Martin reviews the early years of LIFE, when he was literary editor.

Masson, Thomas L. "The Man Who Made 'Life': A Reminiscent Story of John Ames Mitchell." BOOKMAN, 48 (1919), 695.

Masson relates briefly the personality, ideas, and policies of LIFE's founder and first editor.

Mott, Frank Luther. "Fifty Years of LIFE: The Story of a Satirical Weekly." JOURNALISM QUARTERLY, 25 (1948), 224-32.

Mott traces the history of LIFE from its founding, through the changes of editorship subsequent to the death of John Ames Mitchell in 1918, to 1936, when its substantial subscription list was turned over to PUCK, its chief rival.

Smith, James Steel. "LIFE Looks at Literature." AMERICAN LITERATURE, 27 (1958), 23-42.

Smith examines the periodical's photographic essay technique and the literary views and policies expressed throughout its career.

McNAUGHT'S MONTHLY (1924-27)

Monteiro, George. "McNAUGHT'S MONTHLY: Addenda to the Bibliographies of Cather, Dickinson, Fitzgerald, Ford, Hemingway, Hergesheimer and Machen." PAPERS OF THE BIBLIOGRAPHICAL SOCIETY OF AMERICA, 68 (1974), 64-65.

"In its respectable, if modest, run of forty-three issues, McNAUGHT'S managed to attract many distinguished contributors." Eighteen items are listed.

THE NEW YORKER (1925-current)

Adams, Samuel Hopkins. A. WOOLLCOTT: HIS LIFE AND WORLD. New York: Reynal & Hitchcock, 1945.

Chapter XVI, "The Gila Monster," covers Woollcott's stormy term on the NEW YORKER beginning in 1929. Editor Ross had assigned associate editor Katharine S. White the task of dealing with the temperamental writer. "It is regarded in the office as an all but incredible testimonial to diplomacy, firmness, and God-like patience that for nearly ten years Mrs. White was able to handle the 'Gila Monster' (one of Ross' less exasperated characterizations of him) without open rupture."

Bernstein, Burton. THURBER: A BIOGRAPHY. New York: Dodd, Mead, 1975.

Information on Thurber's relationship with the NEW YORKER is included in chapter IX, "Arriving," and following chapters.

Churchill, Allen. "Harold Ross: Editor of THE NEW YORKER." COSMOPOLITAN, 124 (May 1948), 46-47, 174-78.

Churchill begins with an anecdotal portrait of Ross, and then briefly relates Ross's career and the history of the periodical. The article concludes by revealing Ross's regret that less and less humor was appearing in the NEW YORKER.

Drewry, John E. "A Study of NEW YORKER Profiles of Famous Journalists." JOURNALISM QUARTERLY, 23 (1946), 370-80.

Drewry discusses the NEW YORKER "Profile" as a literary form, and the time and care spent on "Profiles" by the NEW YORKER staff. He then lists the 112 "Profiles" of journalists which appeared in the periodical from 1925 to 1945.

Fadiman, Clifton, ed. PROFILES FROM _THE NEW YORKER._ New York: Alfred A. Knopf, 1938.

In his preface (pp. v-ix) Fadiman argues that the NEW YORKER "Profile" is a "form of composition no less specific than the familiar essay, the sonnet, the one-act play."

55 SHORT STORIES FROM THE _NEW YORKER_. New York: Simon & Schuster, 1949.

A brief foreword notes, "The stories in this volume, selected from those that have appeared in THE NEW YORKER during the past ten years, are, the editors believe, representative of the magazine's fiction for that period."

Gill, Brendan. HERE AT THE NEW YORKER. New York: Random House, 1975.

Gill, a writer for the NEW YORKER for forty years, presents a detailed and witty portrait of the editors, artists, and writers who have been associated with the periodical. Included are his own views of the personalities of founder and editor Harold Ross and his successor, William Shawn. The book is illustrated with photographs and NEW YORKER cartoons.

Grant, Jane. ROSS, THE NEW YORKER AND ME. New York: Reynal, 1968.

Jane Grant, a writer for the NEW YORKER and Ross's wife during the first years of his editorship, paints an intimate and detailed portrait of the man and his periodical.

Harrigan, Anthony. "THE NEW YORKER: A Profile." CATHOLIC WORLD, 174 (1952), 444-47.

The NEW YORKER is attacked for being obsolete and narrow-minded.

Harriman, Margaret Case. THE VICIOUS CIRCLE: THE STORY OF THE ALGONQUIN ROUND TABLE. New York: Rinehart, 1951.

Chapter IX, "The Birth of THE NEW YORKER," relates the founding of the periodical and some anecdotes about the personalities involved in its publication.

______, ed. TAKE THEM UP TENDERLY: A COLLECTION OF PROFILES. New York: Alfred A. Knopf, 1945.

In a foreword (pp. xi-xiii) Harriman describes the careful perusal which manuscripts must undergo before final publication.

Harris, Miller, and Howard Gossage. DEAR MISS AFFERBACH, OR THE POSTMAN HARDLY EVER RINGS 11,342 TIMES. New York: Macmillan, 1962.

This book facetiously views the history of two shirt ads in the NEW YORKER. Pages 179-207 examine the periodical's advertising policies and activities, since "a lot has been written about the magazine's editorial side but scarcely anything about the other two-thirds of the book."

HO HUM: NEWSBREAKS FROM THE NEW YORKER. New York: Farrar & Rinehart, 1931; ANOTHER HO HUM: MORE NEWSBREAKS FROM THE NEW YORKER. New York: Farrar & Rinehart, 1932.

In his foreword to this collection, E.B. White humorously describes the NEW YORKER staff's methods of handling the thousands of clippings of newspaper misprints submitted to them.

Holmes, Charles S. THE CLOCKS OF COLUMBUS: THE LITERARY CAREER OF JAMES THURBER. New York: Atheneum, 1972.

In chapter VI, "THE NEW YORKER: Early Days," Holmes examines Thurber's work on the periodical from 1927 to the mid-1930's. He focuses on the influence of E.B. White and Robert Benchley on Thurber's writing, Thurber's success and enthusiasm when writing pieces for "The Talk of the Town" department, and his struggle against editor Harold Ross's criticisms.

Houghton, Donald Eugene. "THE NEW YORKER: Exponent of a Cosmopolitan Elite." Dissertation, University of Minnesota, 1955.

Houghton portrays the ideal NEW YORKER reader, and explains the outlook of the periodical.

Howland, McClure Meredith. "Ross of the NEW YORKER." MAGAZINE WORLD, 3 (April 1947), 9-11, 21, 23.

Ross's biography is sketched, including the details of the founding of the NEW YORKER.

Hyman, Stanley Edgar. "The Urban NEW YORKER." NEW REPUBLIC, 20 July 1942, pp. 90-92.

Hyman analyzes the NEW YORKER style, epitomized, he feels, by the prose of E.B. White. He then views the periodical's journalistic reporting, fiction, "casuals," and poetry.

Ingersoll, Ralph McAllister. POINT OF DEPARTURE: AN ADVENTURE IN AUTOBIOGRAPHY. New York: Harcourt, Brace & World, 1961.

Part 2 (pp. 161-244) covers Ingersoll's managing editorship of the NEW YORKER from 1925 to 1930, and includes descriptions of Harold Ross, James Thurber, Katharine Sergeant Angell, and E.B. White. Ingersoll quit the NEW YORKER for FORTUNE when he concluded that Ross's creative and daring years were behind him.

Johnson, Robert Owen. AN INDEX TO LITERATURE IN THE NEW YORKER: VOLUMES I-XV, 1925-1940. Metuchen, N.J.: Scarecrow Press, 1969; VOLUMES XVI-XXX, 1940-1955, 1970; VOLUMES XXXI-XLV, 1955-1970, 1971.

Each of these volumes is divided into three sections: "Original Material," "Reviews," and "Name Index."

Kramer, Dale. ROSS AND THE NEW YORKER. Garden City, N.Y.: Doubleday, 1951.

Kramer examines Ross's career in detail, and the early struggle and later success of his periodical. He also examines the careers of other people involved with the NEW YORKER, as in chapter IX, "The Artists," and chapter X, "Big Foursome: Angell-White-Thurber-Gibbs."

Kramer, Dale, and George R. Clark. "Harold Ross and THE NEW YORKER: A Landscape with Figures." HARPER'S, 186 (1943), 510-21.

This article covers Ross's early career, including the founding of the NEW YORKER. Kramer and Clark note that Ross has turned to factual reporting in order to keep the periodical in tune with the interests of the public during war time.

Kramer, Hilton. "Harold Ross's 'New Yorker': Life as a Drawing-Room Comedy." COMMENTARY, 28 (1959), 122-27.

The writer considers Ross to have been "ignorant and vain, often cruel and stupid." Of the NEW YORKER's editorial concept Kramer says, "Altogether, it was a concept of sophistication which at the very start was stilted and phony. It was to be sophistication without any talk of sex, politics, or religion--which is to say, sophistication with the guts removed."

Macdonald, Dwight. "Laugh and Lie Down." PARTISAN REVIEW, 4 (December 1937), 44-53.

Macdonald attacks the NEW YORKER as a periodical of the ruling class, as revealed in its humor, editorials, and advertising: "The NEW YORKER is the last of the great family journals. Its inhibitions stretch from sex to the class struggle. . . . The subjects of its profiles, especially if they are wealthy and powerful, are treated deferentially." Ironically, Macdonald was asked to write for the NEW YORKER soon after the appearance of the article, as he himself related later.

Maloney, Russell. "Anything for a Laugh." WRITING FOR LOVE OR MONEY. Ed. Norman Cousins. New York: Longmans, Green, 1949, pp. 158-66.

In this essay on humor Maloney points out the evolution of the humor in the NEW YORKER casuals, or personal essays, as the periodical became more financially secure and the editors less bohemian. Maloney was on the NEW YORKER's staff from 1934 to 1945.

______. "A Profile of THE NEW YORKER Magazine." SATURDAY REVIEW OF LITERATURE, 30 August 1947, pp. 7-10, 29-32.

Maloney gives his views of Harold Ross, James Thurber, E.B. White, and others associated with the periodical. He humorously reiterates parts of "THE NEW YORKER legend, which is surely the most voluminous body of fact, fiction, and conjecture ever attached to any enterprise." Raymond B. Bowen of the NEW YORKER's advertising department replies in a letter in the SATURDAY REVIEW of September 13, 1947, to correct one of Maloney's circulation statistics.

"THE NEW YORKER." FORTUNE, 10 (August 1934), 73-80, 82, 85-86, 88, 90, 92, 97, 150, 152.

This article relates the periodical's history, including the careers of Harold Ross, E.B. White, Katharine White, James Thurber, and others, and the ways these editors cooperated to produce the periodical. The most important information presented here, however, is an extensive examination of the financial organization, advertising policies, and profit margins, since no other source focuses in such detail on these areas.

THE NEW YORKER BOOK OF POEMS, SELECTED BY THE EDITORS OF THE NEW YORKER. New York: Viking Press, 1969.

"All of the poems here are reprinted in the original versions published in THE NEW YORKER." This 820-page anthology contains verse of all types from throughout the periodical's history.

THE NEW YORKER BOOK OF VERSE: AN ANTHOLOGY OF POEMS FIRST PUBLISHED IN THE NEW YORKER, 1925-1935. New York: Harcourt, Brace, 1935.

These 300 poems were chosen from the 4,000 which appeared in the periodical, and which in turn were chosen from 90,000 submissions.

"'New Yorker' Covers." LIFE, 15 July 1946, pp. 68-72.

Sixteen NEW YORKER covers are reproduced, with brief comments about the artists.

Oberfirst, Robert. "Analysis of a NEW YORKER Short Short Story." WRITER, 58 (1945), 48-50, 64.

Oberfirst analyzes "No Sense of Humor," a story by Babette Rosmond, and draws general conclusions about NEW YORKER fiction. "The short short fiction . . . contains an inimitable brand of humor and satire not found in any other contemporary magazine. The short shorts contain little or no plot but are rich in subtle characterization and end with suggestion and point."

Parker, Dorothy. CONSTANT READER. New York: Viking Press, 1970.

Dorothy Parker wrote the "Constant Reader" column "almost every week from October 1927 through May 1928, and intermittently thereafter until 1933." Thirty-one of the forty-six columns are reprinted here.

Rosmond, Babette. ROBERT BENCHLEY: HIS LIFE AND GOOD TIMES. Garden City, N.Y.: Doubleday, 1970.

Benchley's work as drama editor of the NEW YORKER, beginning in 1929, is covered in chapter XII, "I've Tried to Worry but I Can't."

Sampson, Edward C. E.B. WHITE. New York: Twayne, 1974.

In chapter III, "White, THE NEW YORKER, and the Growth of a Moralist," Sampson relates the effect of the Depression on White's writing while he was working for the periodical.

Shaw, Thomas Shuler. INDEX TO PROFILE SKETCHES IN NEW YORKER MAGAZINE, 1925-1970. 2nd ed., rev. Boston: F.W. Faxon, 1972.

The preface notes that "the PROFILES are indexed in three ways: by subjects whether persons or things; by the occupations or some other identification of the subjects of the sketches; and by the names of the authors of the sketches."

Thurber, James. THE YEARS WITH ROSS. Boston: Little, Brown, 1959.

Thurber, who wrote and drew for the NEW YORKER throughout Ross's editorship, presents a detailed portrait, with an account of Ross's personal life and editorial views. Some of this material first appeared in "The Years with Ross," ATLANTIC, 200 (November 1957), 46-51; (December 1957), 45-50; 201 (January 1958), 63-69; (February 1958), 48-55; (March 1958), 54-62; (April, 1958), 49-54; (May 1958), 47-52; (June 1958), 83-88; 202 (July 1958), 40-45; (August 1958), 51-56.

Trilling, Lionel. "'New Yorker' Fiction." NATION, 11 April 1942, pp. 425-26.

Trilling analyzes the short fiction of a number of NEW YORKER writers, and concludes that "the NEW YORKER publishes along with its more genial contents, with its anecdotes, its comic drawings, and its excellent journalism, a kind of short story the main characteristic of which is its great moral intensity."

Watts, Richard, Jr. "Reporters at Large." NEW REPUBLIC, 25 August 1947, pp. 27-28.

> Watts comments on the distinctive characteristics of NEW YORKER reporting. The periodical's writers enjoy a freedom from the pressure of deadlines, and have an opportunity "to move from contemporary events to history, and from literal realism to the representational."

Weales, Gerald. "Not for the Old Lady in Dubuque." DENVER QUARTERLY, 8 (Summer 1973), 65-83. Also published in THE COMIC IMAGINATION IN AMERICAN LITERATURE. Ed. Louis D. Rubin, Jr. Brunswick, N.J.: Rutgers University Press, 1973, pp. 231-46.

> Weales analyzes the early NEW YORKER humor and discusses the personalities of those who wrote it. He regrets the scarcity of magazine humor today.

Whyte, William H., Jr. "You, Too, Can Write the Casual Style." HARPER'S, 207 (October 1953), 87-89.

> Whyte satirizes the writing style which he feels has been refined principally by NEW YORKER writers: "Generally speaking, the more uneventful it [the subject matter] is, or the more pallid the writer's reaction to it, the better do form and content marry."

## THE NORTH AMERICAN REVIEW (1815-1940)

Drewry, John E. "NORTH AMERICAN REVIEW--America's Oldest Magazine." CONTEMPORARY AMERICAN MAGAZINES: A SELECTED BIBLIOGRAPHY AND REPRINTS OF ARTICLES DEALING WITH VARIOUS PERIODICALS. 3rd ed. Athens: University of Georgia Press, 1938, pp. 49-52.

> Drewry focuses on the editorships of George Harvey (1899-1926) and Walter Mahony (1926-35).

Johnson, Willis Fletcher. GEORGE HARVEY: 'A PASSIONATE PATRIOT.' Boston: Houghton Mifflin, 1929.

> Chapter VIII, "'The North American Review,'" relates Harvey's purchase of the journal in 1899. He served as its nineteenth editor until 1926, when he sold it to Walter Butler Mahony. Although the pages of the REVIEW were open to differing points of view, Harvey "made it for the first time a personal organ." He did this by including articles "By the Editor" on the first pages of each issue.

POET LORE (1889-current)

Barnstorff, Hermann. "German Literature in Translation Published by POET LORE, 1891-1939." MODERN LANGUAGE JOURNAL, 25 (1941), 711-15.

> Barnstorff first briefly relates the history and editorial outlook of POET LORE, and then lists chronologically the German authors and works which appeared in the periodical. He remarks upon "the gradual enlargement of the literary horizon, which POET LORE undertook to perform for its reading public," by publishing literature in many foreign languages.

Bernstein, Melvin H. "The Early Years of POET LORE: 1889-1929." POET LORE, 61 (1966), 9-32. Also published as the introd. to Alice Very, comp., A COMPREHENSIVE INDEX OF POET LORE, VOLUMES 1-58: 1889-1963 (see below).

> Bernstein discusses the founding of POET LORE, its contents, its changing editorial policies, and its publishing history. He points out that "its recurrent editorial talent was for exploring the new, the unfamiliar, the unpublished, the faraway, and the foreign writer who in unilingual America was unapproachable."

Holmes, Frank R. A COMPLETE INDEX: VOLUMES 1-25 OF POET LORE, A MAGAZINE OF LETTERS. Boston: Richard G. Badger, 1916.

> A brief publisher's preface surveys the periodical's early history, and a compiler's note relates information on inconsistencies of pagination.

Porter, Charlotte E. "A Story of POET LORE: With Relation to the Late Helen A. Clarke, One of Its Founders." POET LORE, 37 (1926), 432-53.

> The writer relates her founding of POET LORE with Helen A. Clarke in Philadelphia in 1889, the move to Boston in 1892, and the subsequent sale of the journal in 1903. During that time POET LORE was devoted especially to the study of Shakespeare and Robert Browning.

Very, Alice, comp. A COMPREHENSIVE INDEX OF POET LORE, VOLUMES 1-58: 1889-1963. Boston: Branden Press, 1966.

> This author-title index is introduced by Melvin H. Bernstein's essay (see above).

ST. NICHOLAS (1873-1940, 1943)

Calkins, Earnest Elmo. "'St. Nicholas.'" SATURDAY REVIEW OF LITERATURE,

4 May 1940, pp. 7, 14-15.

Calkins views ST. NICHOLAS's achievements from throughout its career.

Commager, Henry Steele, ed. THE ST. NICHOLAS ANTHOLOGY. New York: Random House, 1948; THE SECOND ST. NICHOLAS ANTHOLOGY. New York: Random House, 1950.

Former ST. NICHOLAS editor Mary Lamberton Becker reminisces about the periodical in an introduction to the first volume (pp. xv-xvii). Commager does the same in the preface (pp. xix-xxi).

Erisman, Fred Raymond. "There Was a Child Went Forth: A Study of ST. NICHOLAS MAGAZINE and Selected Children's Authors, 1890-1915." Dissertation, University of Minnesota, 1966.

Erisman examines the work of Ralph Henry Barbour, Kate Douglas Wiggin, and L. Frank Baum, focusing on the discrepancy between their idealistic fiction and the factual nonfiction published simultaneously in the periodical.

Finletter, Gretchen. "Was This Romance?" ATLANTIC, 174 (August 1944), 57-60.

The writer reveals her childhood interest in the ST. NICHOLAS, and mentions some of its young contributors, among them E. Vincent Millay, S.V. Benet, and Robert Hillyer.

Shaw, John Mackay, comp. THE POEMS, POETS & ILLUSTRATORS OF ST. NICHOLAS MAGAZINE, 1873-1943, AN INDEX. Tallahassee: Florida State University Strozier Library, 1965.

Shaw lists the poems, poets, and illustrators in three separate sections.

THE SATURDAY REVIEW OF LITERATURE (1920-current)

Benet, William Rose. "The Editor Looks at Poetry." WRITING FOR LOVE OR MONEY. Ed. Norman Cousins. New York: Longmans, Green, 1949, pp. 136-43.

The SATURDAY REVIEW's poetry editor relates the periodical's policies and the procedures followed for selecting poetry. Benet also looks back to the policies of "The Literary Review," the SATURDAY REVIEW's predecessor (see next entry).

_____. "The Phoenix Nest." SATURDAY REVIEW OF LITERATURE, 17 June 1933, p. 657; 24 June 1933, p. 669; 1 July 1933, p. 681; 8 July 1933, p. 695.

Benet, who had been with the REVIEW from its inception, traces its history under editor Henry Seidel Canby from its days as the "Book Review" and then "The Literary Review," supplements to the NEW YORK EVENING POST. He examines in detail the contents of the first nine years of the journal, including the changes in format, the arrival of new editors, and the appearance of new departments and columns.

Bennion, Sherilyn Cox. "SATURDAY REVIEW: From Literature to Life." Dissertation, Syracuse University, 1968.

This is a thorough history of the SATURDAY REVIEW, including a section on business operations and advertising.

Canby, Henry Seidel. AMERICAN MEMOIR. Cambridge, Mass.: Houghton Mifflin, 1947.

Canby edited the REVIEW for fifteen years, beginning when it was a newspaper supplement in 1921. In chapter III of part 3, "An Arsenal of Literature," he recounts the transformation of the REVIEW into an independent journal. In chapter IV, "The Passion for Print," he discusses some of the reviewers with whom he came in contact.

Cousins, Norman. PRESENT TENSE: AN AMERICAN EDITOR'S ODYSSEY. New York: McGraw-Hill Book Co., 1967.

Cousins, editor of the journal from 1940, presents incidents and personalities from its history in part 1, "The Life and Times of the SATURDAY REVIEW." The second part reprints editorials Cousins wrote from 1940 to 1967.

______. "Retrospect and Prospect." SATURDAY REVIEW, 5 March 1960, pp. 28-29.

Cousins reviews generally his twenty-year editorship of the journal, including his relationship with owner E. DeGolyer, who disagreed with Cousins philosophically but never interfered with editorial policies.

Cowley, Malcolm. "Dr. Canby and His Team." SATURDAY REVIEW, 29 August 1964, pp. 54-55, 177.

Cowley, who began his association with the REVIEW as a book reviewer in 1924, relates the circumstances of the periodical's founding. The greatest value of the REVIEW, and editor Canby's main purpose, was "to encourage the writing of good books by finding more readers for them."

Fellows of the Library of Congress in American Letters et al. THE CASE AGAINST THE SATURDAY REVIEW OF LITERATURE. Chicago: Poetry, 1949.

In this eighty-page pamphlet, a number of poets and critics, including Allen Tate and Malcolm Cowley, counter the SATURDAY REVIEW's criticism of those who awarded the Bollingen Prize to Ezra Pound in 1949.

Marshall, Margaret. "'The Saturday Review' Unfair to Literature." NATION, 17 December 1949, pp. 598-99.

This article attacks the REVIEW for its criticism of the awarding of the Bollingen Prize to Ezra Pound. It is followed by a protest letter, signed by a number of writers, which the REVIEW had itself refused to print.

THE SATURDAY REVIEW OF LITERATURE: INDEX 1924-1944. New York: R.R. Bowker, 1971.

This index includes "all articles, editorials, reviews, departments, notes, and fillers.

THE SATURDAY REVIEW TREASURY; A VOLUME OF GOOD READING SELECTED FROM THE COMPLETE FILES BY JOHN HAVERSTICK AND THE EDITORS OF THE SATURDAY REVIEW. New York: Simon & Schuster, 1957.

In an introduction to this anthology, Joseph Wood Krutch presents a brief account of the journal's founding and history (pp. xvii-xxv).

SCRIBNER'S MAGAZINE (1886-1937)

Allen, Frederick Lewis. "Fifty Years of SCRIBNER'S MAGAZINE." SCRIBNER'S, 101 (January 1937), 17-24.

In the second half of his article Allen discusses the changes in content made by SCRIBNER'S in order to compete successfully with the new, cheaper magazines.

Burlingame, Roger. OF MAKING MANY BOOKS: A HUNDRED YEARS OF READING, WRITING AND PUBLISHING. New York: Charles Scribner's Sons, 1946.

Chapter XIII, "The Magazine," covers the history of SCRIBNER'S from its founding in 1886 through the editorships of Edward Burlingame (1886-1914), Robert Bridges (1914-30), and finally Alfred Dashiell (1930-37). Chapters XIV and XV, "Pictures" and "Poetry," contain information on the periodical's use of illustrations and its editorial policies.

Drewry, John E. "SCRIBNER'S--A Magazine Interested in the Unusual." CONTEMPORARY AMERICAN MAGAZINES: A SELECTED BIBLIOGRAPHY AND REPRINTS OF ARTICLES DEALING WITH VARIOUS PERIODICALS. 3rd ed. Athens: University of Georgia Press, 1938, pp. 67-69.

Drewry focuses on the editorial policies of SCRIBNER'S in the late 1920's and early 1930's.

Holman, C. Hugh. "Thomas Wolfe, SCRIBNER'S MAGAZINE, and 'The Blest NOUVELLE.'" ESSAYS MOSTLY ON PERIODICAL PUBLISHING IN AMERICA: A COLLECTION IN HONOR OF CLARENCE GOHDES. Ed. James Woodress. Durham, N.C.: Duke University Press, 1973, pp. 205-20.

In SCRIBNER'S MAGAZINE, under the editorship of Alfred Dashiell from 1930 to 1936, "Wolfe, somewhat like Henry James and THE YELLOW BOOK, was fortunate in having available to him the pages of a magazine interested in the short novel and anxious to give it audience."

Meriwether, James B. "Faulkner's Correspondence with SCRIBNER'S MAGAZINE." PROOF, 3 (1973), 253-82.

THE SMART SET (1900-1930)

Angoff, Charles. "The Mystique of THE SMART SET." LITERARY REVIEW, 11 (1967), 46-60.

Angoff reviews the history of the SMART SET and its importance for literary journalism. He praises Willard Huntington Wright, editor in 1913 and 1914, whose transformation of the SMART SET into a frank, quality literary periodical "was nothing less than a journalistic revolution," although he has been overshadowed by H.L. Mencken and George Jean Nathan, who usurped his position. Angoff criticizes Carl Dolmetsch for not seeing Wright's importance (see Dolmetsch's works, below).

Cowley, Malcolm. "The SMART SET Legend." NEW REPUBLIC, 16 January 1935, p. 281.

In this book review Cowley challenges Burton Rascoe's assertion in THE SMART SET ANTHOLOGY (cited below) that Mencken and Nathan were editorial pioneers.

Dolmetsch, Carl R[ichard]. "History of the SMART SET Magazine, 1914-1923." Dissertation, University of Chicago, 1957.

_____. "Mencken as a Magazine Editor." MENCKENIANA, 21 (Spring 1967), 1-8.

Dolmetsch discusses the achievements of Mencken as SMART SET editor. So much attention has been focused on his other pursuits that "the real significance of Mencken the workaday magazine editor has been at least partially obscured."

_____. THE SMART SET: A HISTORY AND ANTHOLOGY. New York: Dial Press, 1966.

This ninety-one-page history examines in detail the editorial policies of Willard Huntington Wright (1913-14), H.L. Mencken and George Jean Nathan (1914-23), Morris Gilbert (1924), and George D'Utassey (1924-25). The relationship of the SMART SET to many of its most famous contributors, including F. Scott Fitzgerald and Eugene O'Neill, is explored, as well as the periodical's rivalries with publications such as AINSLEE'S, which imitated it, and COLLIER'S. Dolmetsch notes that James Playsted Wood's MAGAZINES IN THE UNITED STATES "unfortunately abounds in factual errors about THE SMART SET, as do all other reference books which mention the magazine."

Mencken, H[enry] L[ouis]. H.L. MENCKEN'S SMART SET CRITICISM. Ed. William H. Nolte. Ithaca, N.Y.: Cornell University Press, 1968.

In the editor's introduction, before beginning an analysis of Mencken's literary theories, Nolte explains how Mencken began his fifteen-year association with the SMART SET through the help of Theodore Dreiser.

_____. A PERSONAL WORD. New York: Smart Set, 1922.

This sixteen-page promotional pamphlet reviews the history of the SMART SET under Mencken and George Jean Nathan's editorship.

Nolte, William H. "THE SMART SET: Mencken for the Defense." SOUTH DAKOTA REVIEW, 6 (Autumn 1968), 3-11.

Nolte discusses Mencken's editorial abilities, especially his rapport with contributors. He also concludes that "more than any other single magazine, THE SMART SET cleared the way for an aesthetic approach to art free from moralistic dogma."

Rascoe, Burton. "'Smart Set' History." THE SMART SET ANTHOLOGY. Ed. Burton Rascoe and Groff Conklin. New York: Reynal & Hitchcock, 1934, pp. xiii-xliv.

One of Rascoe's major points in this detailed history is that much more literature of value was published during Willard Huntington Wright's editorship than has generally been recognized, because of the prominence of his successors. He specifically criticizes Isaac Goldberg's THE MAN MENCKEN: A BIOGRAPHICAL AND

CRITICAL SURVEY on this score. This introduction was published in advance as a booklet, SMART SET HISTORY (New York: Reynal and Hitchcock, 1934). The printing was limited to 750 copies.

See also studies by Bode, Goldberg, Kemler, Manchester, Mayfield, Nathan, Simpson, Stenerson, and Mencken's LETTERS, listed in the General Studies section of this chapter, above.

TOMORROW (1941-51)

Hagemann, E.R. "A Selected Check-List of TOMORROW, 1941-1951." BULLETIN OF BIBLIOGRAPHY, 24 (1966), 216-24, 234-40; 25 (1966), 17-24.

Editor and founder Eileen J. Garrett published work by new as well as established writers. Hagemann places the periodical "in the tradition of the journals in American cultural affairs, e.g., NORTH AMERICAN REVIEW, CENTURY, SCRIBNER'S and INDEPENDENT, and indeed [it] was the last of its kind."

UNPARTIZAN REVIEW (1914, 1919-21), entitled UNPOPULAR REVIEW (1914-19)

Madison, Charles A. THE OWL AMONG COLOPHONS: HENRY HOLT AS PUBLISHER AND EDITOR. New York: Holt, Rinehart and Winston, 1966.

Chapter XI, "Holt's Periodical Publications," covers the publisher's founding and support of the REVIEW until 1921, when "postwar inflation and his great age combined to force its suspension."

Warren, George T. "The Mercury Idea." MENCKENIANA, 47 (Fall 1973), 25-26.

Warren speculates that "Henry Holt's UNPOPULAR REVIEW could have started sowing the seed that later brought forth the AMERICAN MERCURY with its iconoclastic articles and stories calculated to jolt members of the Establishment out of their easy chairs."

VANITY FAIR (1914-36)

Amory, Cleveland, and Frederic Bradlee, eds. VANITY FAIR, SELECTIONS FROM AMERICA'S MOST MEMORABLE MAGAZINE: A CAVALCADE OF THE 1920'S AND 1930'S. New York: Viking Press, 1960.

Amory begins this illustrated collection with "Introduction--A Fair Kept" (pp. 7-9), in which he reviews the history of VANITY

FAIR, focusing on editor Frank Crowninshield's literary discoveries and the quality of his staff. Bradlee follows this with a profile, "Frank Crowninshield--Editor, Man, and Uncle" (pp. 11-12). Also included is an excerpt from the first issue's editorial, published in March 1914, stating VANITY FAIR's goals (p. 13).

Drewry, John E. "VANITY FAIR--The Sophisticated Magazine." CONTEMPORARY AMERICAN MAGAZINES--A SELECTED BIBLIOGRAPHY AND REPRINTS OF ARTICLES DEALING WITH VARIOUS PERIODICALS. 3rd ed. Athens: University of Georgia Press, 1938, pp. 70-71.

Drewry briefly discusses the contents of VANITY FAIR. He sees the periodical as a projection of the personality of editor Frank Crowninshield.

Laverty, Carroll D. "VANITY FAIR: The Voice of the Twenties." JOURNAL OF THE AMERICAN STUDIES ASSOCIATION OF TEXAS, 3 (1972), 14-20.

Meine, F.J. "VANITY FAIR." COLLEGE JOURNALISM, 4 (1934), 461-63.

# Chapter 4

# LITTLE MAGAZINES OF POETRY, FICTION, AND ART

## GENERAL STUDIES

Allen, Charles. "The Advance Guard." SEWANEE REVIEW, 51 (1943), 410-29.

Allen emphasizes the importance of little magazines in introducing new writers who otherwise would be unable to publish. He relates the history of the New Orleans DOUBLE DEALER to show the spirit of experimentation typical of these periodicals.

_____. "'The Advance Guard': A Chapter in the History of the American Little Magazine." Dissertation, University of Iowa, 1943.

_____. "American Little Magazines, 1912-1944." INDIANA QUARTERLY FOR THE BOOKMAN, 1 (April 1945), 45-54.

This article surveys the little magazine movement.

_____. "GLEBE and OTHERS." COLLEGE ENGLISH, 5 (1944), 418-23.

Alfred Kreymbourg founded GLEBE in 1913 and edited it until 1915, and then founded and guided OTHERS from 1915 intermittently until its last issue in 1919. Among the poets whose careers these periodicals helped to launch were William Carlos Williams, Marianne Moore, and Wallace Stevens.

Alpert, Barry Stephen. "The Unexamined Art: Ezra Pound and the Aesthetic Mode of the Little Magazine." Dissertation, Stanford University, 1971.

Alpert studies Pound's involvement with and influence upon little magazines from 1909 to 1928.

AMERICAN WRITING. THE ANTHOLOGY AND YEARBOOK OF THE AMERICAN NON-COMMERCIAL MAGAZINE. 1942-43 yearbooks ed. Alan Swallow. Prairie City, Ill.: J.A. Decker, 1943, 1944; 1944 yearbook ed. Helen Ferguson

Caukin and Alan Swallow. Boston: Bruce Humphries, 1945.

Included in the yearbook section of these anthologies are "honor rolls" of stories and poems, and lists of little magazines which published the greatest number of high-quality contributions.

Ball, Roland C., Jr. "Literary Criticism and Theory in the American Little Magazines." Dissertation, University of California, Berkeley, 1953.

Barbour, Thomas. "Little Magazines in Paris." HUDSON REVIEW, 4 (1951), 278-83.

After reviewing NEW STORY, ID, JANUS, ZERO, and POINTS, all published by Americans, Barbour concludes that the quality of writing and editing is worse than that produced by the expatriates of the 1920's.

Bernstein, David. "The Little Magazines." SCHOLASTIC, 13 October 1934, pp. 10, 13.

Bernstein lists some of the current little magazines and provides a general introduction to the field.

Bixler, Paul. "Little Magazine, What Now?" ANTIOCH REVIEW, 8 (1948), 63-77.

Bixler challenges the definition of the genre given by Hoffman, Allen, and Ulrich in THE LITTLE MAGAZINE: A HISTORY AND A BIBLIOGRAPHY (see below). He considers it a mistake to limit the genre primarily to those magazines of the purely literary avant-garde. "It is characteristic of the authors that they chose the year and the appearance of POETRY [1912] rather than of THE MASSES [1911] to fix the movement."

Bridson, D.G. "Foreign Reviews: American Periodicals." CRITERION, 14 (1935), 722-29.

Bridson regrets the demise of HOUND & HORN, because now no literary journal exists "in which left and right, humanistic and humanitarian, can rub shoulders in creation of literature valuable as one or another form of art." He also reviews the contents and current outlooks of other periodicals, including the AMERICAN REVIEW, the MODERN MONTHLY, and POETRY.

Burgess, Gelett. BAYSIDE BOHEMIA: FIN DE SIECLE SAN FRANCISCO & ITS LITTLE MAGAZINES. San Francisco: Book Club of California, 1954.

Burgess includes brief chapters on the LARK, LE PETIT JOURNAL DES REFUSEES, the WAVE, and PHYLLIDA; OR, THE MILKMAID, all published just before 1900.

Cantwell, Robert. "The Little Magazines." NEW REPUBLIC, 25 July 1934, pp. 295-97.

The writer notes the proliferation of new publications since 1932 and reviews the contents of a number of them.

Cowley, Malcolm. "The Little Magazines Growing Up." NEW YORK TIMES BOOK REVIEW, 14 September 1947, pp. 5, 35.

Cowley compares the little magazines of the 1920's to those of the 1940's and concludes that "it might as well be flatly said that the little magazines of today are better edited and better written than their predecessors."

______. "Ten Little Magazines." NEW REPUBLIC, 31 March 1947, pp. 30-33.

This article analyzes the editorial content and policies of each of the following publications: ACCENT, CHIMERA, POETRY, KENYON REVIEW, FURIOSO, QUARTERLY REVIEW OF LITERATURE, the WESTERN REVIEW, the SEWANEE REVIEW, POLITICS, and PARTISAN REVIEW. Cowley concludes that all "deserve to be more widely known."

Dillon, George. "The 'Little Magazine' Gimmick." POETRY, 71 (1947), 41-44.

Dillon discusses generally the role of little magazines in postwar America and Europe.

D[obree], B[onamy]. "Foreign Periodicals: American Periodicals." CRITERION, 10 (1931), 587-92.

This article reviews the contents and editorial policies of a number of periodicals, including SYMPOSIUM and HOUND & HORN, and less well known journals ARGO, BLUES, HESPERIAN, and CONTEMPORARY VISION.

Duffey, Bernard. THE CHICAGO RENAISSANCE IN AMERICAN LETTERS. 1954; rpt. Westport, Conn.: Greenwood Press, 1972.

Chapter X of part 2, "Three Voices of Liberation," reveals the contributions of Floyd Dell of the FRIDAY LITERARY REVIEW, Harriet Monroe of POETRY, and Margaret Anderson of the LITTLE REVIEW to the Chicago renaissance during the second decade of the twentieth century.

F.,W.J. "Innocents Abroad." DOUBLE DEALER, 4 (1922), 201-4.

The writer endeavors to "pass final judgment on the fledglings" BROOM, GARGOYLE, and SECESSION, with results uncomplimentary to the periodicals and their editors.

GALLEY; THE LITTLE MAGAZINE QUARTERLY. North Hollywood, Calif.: Proof, 1949-53.

This publication appeared irregularly and with various subtitles. The first issue (Spring 1949) contains a little magazine directory which is "the most comprehensive list published" (pp. 4-21). It includes locations, founding dates, editors, and general policy statements. A statistical survey and list of editors follow (pp. 22-25). Other issues contain information on advertising rates, little magazine publishers, little magazine presses, and related subjects.

Greenberg, Clement. "The Renaissance of the Little Mag." PARTISAN REVIEW, 8 (1941), 72-76.

Greenberg reviews the contents of the following new little magazines: ACCENT, DIOGENES, EXPERIMENTAL REVIEW, VICE VERSA, and VIEW. He criticizes them for their purposelessness and feels that their writers should be more politically oriented. "And as for their poetry--it will need less than now to be journalistic and modish in order to be pertinent."

Guenther, Paul, and Nicholas Joost. "Little Magazines and the Cosmopolitan Tradition." PAPERS ON LANGUAGE AND LITERATURE, 6 (1970), 100-110.

The authors discuss the cultural significance of little magazines between the world wars, focusing on DER QUERSCHNITT in Germany and the DIAL and the SEVEN ARTS in America.

Hall, Donald. MARIANNE MOORE: THE CAGE AND THE ANIMAL. New York: Pegasus, 1970.

Chapter III, "OTHERS," covers Moore's association with Alfred Kreymbourg, his periodical, and the literary group which met at his country home in New Jersey. Chapter V, "THE DIAL," covers Moore's editorship of that journal from 1925 until it ceased publication in 1929. Hall discusses her strict editorial standards and the relationships she consequently had with various writers and poets.

Hemingway, Ernest. A MOVEABLE FEAST. New York: Charles Scribner's Sons, 1964.

In "The Man Who Was Marked for Death" (pp. 121-29), Hemingway implies duplicity on the part of Ernest Walsh, coeditor of THIS QUARTER, for promising the journal's literary award, which never materialized, to James Joyce, Ezra Pound, and Hemingway himself. He also implies that Walsh had a special arrangement with the DIAL for publishing his own poetry. For the debate over Hemingway's accuracy and fairness, see William Wasserstrom, "Hemingway, the DIAL, and Ernest Walsh," SOUTH ATLANTIC QUARTERLY, 65 (1966), 171-77, and Nicholas Joost, "Ernest Hemingway and THE DIAL," NEOPHILOLOGUS, 5 (1968), 180-90, 304-13.

Hoffman, Frederick J. "The Little Magazines: Portrait of an Age." SATURDAY REVIEW OF LITERATURE, 25 December 1943, pp. 3-5.

This article investigates how the little magazine "accomodated itself to the search for values and to the experiments with form which must be considered the principal contributions of the early twentieth century to literary history."

______. "Little Magazines and the Avant-Garde." ART IN SOCIETY, 1 (Fall 1960), 32-37.

After discussing the general characteristics of little magazines, Hoffman compares those published from 1915 to 1930, which were "on their own," to those published after World War II, which were sponsored by universities and foundations.

______. "Research Value of the 'Little Magazine.'" COLLEGE AND RESEARCH LIBRARIES, 6 (1945), 311-16.

Citing Hart Crane's association with PAGANY as an example, Hoffman considers the important role played by little magazines in the early careers of many important writers. He also discusses generally the motivations behind these periodicals and the characteristics which differentiate them from other publications.

Hoffman, Frederick J.; Charles Allen; and Carolyn F. Ulrich. THE LITTLE MAGAZINE: A HISTORY AND A BIBLIOGRAPHY. 1946; rpt. New York: Kraus Reprint, 1967.

This comprehensive history examines developments in the field from before World War I to the end of World War II. Detailed editing and publishing histories are given for the following journals: POETRY, OTHERS, the LITTLE REVIEW, the SEVEN ARTS, SECESSION, BROOM, the DIAL, the FUGITIVE, TRANSITION, the MIDLAND, HOUND & HORN. A 134-page bibliography contains publishing information and a one- or two-paragraph annotation for each entry.

The following journals receive substantial examination: 1911: The MASSES, the WESTMINSTER MAGAZINE; 1917: The QUILL, the SANSCULOTTE; 1918: The LIBERATOR; 1919: S4N; 1920: CONTACT, the FRONTIER; 1921: The DOUBLE DEALER, VOICES; 1922: LAUGHING HORSE; 1923: The MODERN QUARTERLY; 1925: THIS QUARTER; 1926: The NEW MASSES, TWO WORLDS MONTHLY; 1927: BOZART; 1929: The GYROSCOPE; 1930: The HARKNESS HOOT; 1931: The LEFT, STORY; 1932: The AMERICAN SPECTATOR, TREND; 1933: The ANVIL, the LITTLE MAGAZINE, 1933; 1934: HINTERLAND, LITERARY AMERICA, MANU-

SCRIPT, PARTISAN REVIEW, the UNIVERSITY REVIEW; 1935: AMERICAN PREFACES; 1937: DIRECTION, INTERMOUNTAIN REVIEW OF ENGLISH AND SPEECH; 1938: The LITTLE MAN, the PHOENIX, TWICE A YEAR; 1939: FURIOSO; 1940: ACCENT; 1941: DECISION; 1942: The CHIMERA; 1944: MARYLAND QUARTERLY.

A supplementary list of other periodicals includes substantial examinations of the following: 1910: The YALE LITERARY MAGAZINE; 1912: The SMART SET; 1915: The HARVARD ADVOCATE, the TEXAS REVIEW; 1919: The AMERICAN POETRY MAGAZINE; 1929: FOLK-SAY; 1930: The NEW MEXICO QUARTERLY; 1935: The SOUTHERN REVIEW; 1939: The KENYON REVIEW.

Ignatow, David. "L.C. Woodman: A Personal Memory." CARLETON MISCELLANY, 6 (Summer 1965), 47-69.

Ignatow remembers the tragic failings of Lawrence Woodman's teaching career and personal life. Woodman edited and mimeographed LITERARY ARTS, AMERICAN SCENE, IDIOM, and WOMANKIND, and his activities and ambitions as an editor are discussed here.

______. "Unfinished Business. . . ." CARLETON MISCELLANY, 6 (Winter 1965), 69-74.

Lawrence Woodman, founder of a number of short-lived journals in the 1930's, helped Ignatow finance his own literary periodical, ANALYTIC, in 1937. This article recalls Ignatow's journalistic association with Woodman. It also examines the difference in outlook during the 1930's between the Marxist writers on journals such as the ANVIL and the NEW MASSES and the liberals who wrote for the ATLANTIC, HARPER'S, and other established periodicals.

Janssens, G.A. "THE DIAL and THE SEVEN ARTS." PAPERS ON LANGUAGE AND LITERATURE, 4 (1968), 442-58.

Janssens argues that the similarities between the SEVEN ARTS and the DIAL have been exaggerated. The earlier journal called for the development of a national culture, but the later one was international in outlook. In addition, the DIAL's admiration for members of the SEVEN ARTS group declined steadily in the 1920's. This material was taken from Janssens's THE AMERICAN LITERARY REVIEW: A CRITICAL HISTORY 1920-1950, cited in chapter 11.

Johnson, Abby Ann Arthur, and Ronald M. Johnson. "Forgotten Pages: Black Literary Magazines in the 1920's." JOURNAL OF AMERICAN STUDIES, 8 (1974), 363-82.

This article relates the publishing histories and editorial policies of the following little magazines: FIRE (Harlem, 1926, one issue),

HARLEM (1928, one issue), BLACK OPALS (Philadelphia, 1927-28), SATURDAY EVENING QUILL (Boston, 1928-30). Other black journals are also mentioned in the course of this article.

Joost, Nicholas. "THE DIAL, THE LITTLE REVIEW and the New Movement." MIDCONTINENT AMERICAN STUDIES JOURNAL, 8 (Spring 1967), 44-59.

This article examines the relationship, at times the rivalry, between these journals in the early 1920's: "The cooler and more cautious DIAL reaped the benefits of its colleague's pugnacity--and soon earned in its turn the animosity of the more daring journal."

_____. ERNEST HEMINGWAY AND THE LITTLE MAGAZINES: THE PARIS YEARS. Barre, Mass.: Barre Publishers, 1968.

This detailed study includes separate chapters on Hemingway's association early in his career with the DOUBLE DEALER, POETRY, the LITTLE REVIEW, and THIS QUARTER, as well as his editorship of Ford Madox Ford's TRANSATLANTIC REVIEW. The first chapter (pp. 1-15) and the epilogue (pp. 155-66) discuss Hemingway's early rejection by the DIAL and his resulting bitterness which Joost feels was misdirected.

Josephson, Matthew. LIFE AMONG THE SURREALISTS. New York: Holt, Rinehart and Winston, 1962.

In chapter IX, "How to Start a Literary Movement," Josephson tells about his founding of SECESSION with Gorham Munson in Vienna in 1922, as well as his involvement with Harold Loeb's BROOM, first brought out in Rome. Chapter XIII, "'The Poet's Return,'" covers BROOM's removal to New York in 1923, Josephson's struggle to keep it alive economically, his infamous fistfight with Munson (differing from Munson's version), and the censorship of the last, the January 1924, issue of BROOM by the U.S. Post Office.

Kaplan, Philip. Untitled article. MAINSTREAM, 15 (November 1962), 31-32.

Kaplan briefly views the history of the little magazine from the 1920's through World War II.

Kees, Weldon. "Magazine Chronicle." PRAIRIE SCHOONER, 13 (1939), 66-69.

Kees regrets the demise of left-wing magazines, including CONTACT, CONTEMPO, SPACE, ANVIL, and BLAST. He hopes for a new magazine "appearing regularly and often enough, devoted chiefly to creative work, with metropolitan aims." The PRAIRIE SCHOONER editors reply by questioning the value of experimental tendenz magazines and pointing out the health and longevity of their own publication as well as those of the SOUTHWEST REVIEW and the FRONTIER-MIDLAND. A reply to this reply by E.G. Arnold appears in the next issue, 13 (1939), 135-36.

Knox, George. "Idealism, Vagabondage, Socialism: Charles A. Sandburg in TO-MORROW and the FRA." HUNTINGTON LIBRARY QUARTERLY, 38 (1975), 161-88.

Knox examines Charles [Carl] Sandburg's contributions to the free-thinking socialist journal TO-MORROW and to Elbert Hubbard's FRA between 1905 and 1910, an important period in Sandburg's early poetic development.

Kramer, Dale. CHICAGO RENAISSANCE: THE LITERARY LIFE IN THE MID-WEST: 1900-1930. New York: Appleton-Century, 1966.

The following chapters cover literary periodicals: VIII, "FRIDAY LITERARY REVIEW--Dell and a Brash Young Irishman"; XV, "Harriet Monroe: POETRY's Muse"; XVIII, "Margaret Anderson and the LITTLE REVIEW."

Kreymbourg, Alfred. TROUBADOUR: AN AUTOBIOGRAPHY. New York: Boni and Liveright, 1925.

Part 3, "OTHERS," relates Kreymbourg's founding and editing of GLEBE and then OTHERS. Chapters VIII through X of part 4, "BROOM," "America in Europe," and "The Eternal Past," present details of the founding of BROOM in Rome by Kreymbourg and Harold Loeb, a venture from which the author withdrew after a year. Also, chapters III and IV of part 2, "An Editorial Dream" and "Tobogganing," cover Kreymbourg's abortive first attempt to found a literary periodical which was to have been entitled the AMERICAN QUARTERLY.

Laughlin, James IV. "The 'Little Mags': 1934." HARKNESS HOOT, 4 (April 1934), 41-48.

Laughlin concludes his evaluation by stating that "one need only read through a few copies of STORY to realize that the average of serious prose is far higher than it has ever been before, while STORY's phenomenal popularity is indicative of an increase in the body of discriminating readers."

Lindeman, Jack. Untitled article. MAINSTREAM, 15 (December 1962), 37-38.

The editor of WHETSTONE retrospectively views the importance of little magazines, and offers a definition of the type. Aside from matters of economics and circulation, an important factor is that "the little mag . . . operates strictly according to the personal tastes and prejudices of the editor or editors implying a 'take it or leave it' concern for its audience."

"Little Mags, What Now?" NEW REPUBLIC, 31 March 1941, p. 424.

This short article provides brief sketches of the following new little magazines: DECISION, VIEW, NEW HORIZONS, MATRIX, DIRECTION, VICE VERSA, ACCENT, DIOGENES, and VOICES.

McAlmon, Robert, and Kay Boyle. BEING GENIUSES TOGETHER, 1920-1930. Garden City, N.Y.: Doubleday, 1968.

These personal accounts of the literary scene in the 1920's, primarily among expatriates in Europe, include information on a number of little magazines and their editors. TRANSITION and THIS QUARTER are discussed most extensively. This loosely organized book includes a useful index.

Mayer, Stanley Dehler. "The Poetry Magazines." SCHOLASTIC, 23 March 1935, pp. 6, 13.

Mayer discusses the general role of contemporary poetry magazines, lists some of them, and comments on their individual policies.

Munson, Gorham. "Greenwich Village That Was: Seedbed of the Nineteen-Twenties." LITERARY REVIEW, 5 (1962), 313-35.

Included in this reminiscence about the Village and its personalities is a discussion of the PAGAN, started by Joseph Kling in 1916. Kling gave Hart Crane his start, but when the poet graduated to the LITTLE REVIEW, he turned on Kling and accused him of publishing a "fetid corpse" of a magazine.

_____. "How to Run a Little Magazine." SATURDAY REVIEW OF LITERATURE, 27 March 1937, pp. 3-4, 14, 16-17.

The former editor of SECESSION facetiously advises any prospective little-magazine proprietor on the problems of publication, from the planning of the first issue to the inevitable death of the venture.

_____. "Interstice between Scylla and Charybdis." SECESSION, no. 2 (July 1922), pp. 30-32.

Munson describes two classifications of literary review--the personal, including the LITTLE REVIEW, and the anthological, a less interesting type, including BROOM. He then states that "SECESSION aims to be neither . . . but to be a group organ." The group it speaks for consists of unknown, path-breaking artists.

Norman, Charles. EZRA POUND. New York: Funk & Wagnalls, 1969.

Pound's work for POETRY is covered in chapter V, "POETRY's Foreign Correspondent." He encouraged the LITTLE REVIEW and the DIAL as well, and helped them to find contributors. His relationship with these journals is traced throughout this biography.

O'Brien, Edward J. "The Little Magazines." VANITY FAIR, 41 (October 1933), 20-21, 58.

O'Brien notes in this survey that for twenty years following the initial burst of activity in the 1890's, few new publications were started because writers viewed themselves more as established businessmen than avant-garde nonconformist artists, and therefore didn't support such ventures.

O'Connor, William Van. "The Direction of the Little Magazine." POETRY, 71 (1948), 281-84.

O'Connor reviews the stated editorial policies of three new little magazines, EPOCH, TOUCHSTONE, and STATESIDE. He supports their policies of limiting their interest to specific fields of literature, since this avoids unnecessary competition.

______. "Little Magazines in the Third Generation." POETRY, 73 (1949), 367-69.

The little magazines of the 1940's "find themselves in the position of having to refine upon or restate the position of their fathers." O'Connor surveys the new crop, including CONTEMPORARY POETRY, CONTOUR, AMERICAN LETTERS, INTERIM, the WIND AND THE RAIN, and VARIEGATION: A FREE VERSE QUARTERLY.

______. "New Magazines, Here and Abroad." POETRY, 71 (1947), 104-7.

Included in this survey of new publications are DEATH, "not dissimilar in tone from BROOM," and MAINSTREAM, a Marxist publication. O'Connor sees similarities between the new journals and their predecessors in earlier decades.

______. "Recent Magazines: The Expense of Conventions." POETRY, 76 (1950), 118-20.

New little magazines such as the QUARTERLY REVIEW OF LITERATURE should be welcomed because they publish unknown writers. Other journals, such as the HUDSON REVIEW, have patterned themselves after established periodicals and publish well-known writers.

Pollak, Felix. "Landing in Little Magazines--Capturing(?) a Trend." ARIZONA QUARTERLY, 19 (1963), 101-15.

Pollak reviews the role of little magazines in the past, conjectures on their future, and concludes that they "are among the few barriers against the all too common denominators established by the majority in its own image, and against the totalitarianism of standards set by the famous (but undistinguished) man in the street."

______. "The World of the Little Magazines." ARTS IN SOCIETY, 2 (Spring-Summer 1962), 49-66.

This article includes editorial manifestos from the LITTLE REVIEW, POETRY, TRANSITION, the FUGITIVE, and later publications CONTACT, the FIFTIES, and BEATITUDE. Pollak also discusses the development of new writers and new cultural ideas in little magazines.

Pound, Ezra. THE LETTERS OF EZRA POUND, 1907-1941. Ed. D.D. Paige. New York: Harcourt, Brace, 1950.

Section I of "Part One: London (1907-1920)," entitled "POETRY: A MAGAZINE OF VERSE," includes letters sent to Harriet Monroe, one of which urges her to publish T.S. Eliot's "The Love Song of J. Alfred Prufrock" (pp. 50-51). Section II, "THE LITTLE REVIEW," reveals Pound's close association with Margaret Anderson's journal. He wanted her to guarantee regular publication of his, Eliot's, James Joyce's, and Wyndham Lewis's work (pp. 106-7).

______. "Small Magazines." ENGLISH JOURNAL, 19 (1930), 689-704.

After reviewing the history of little magazines, Pound concludes that they have been leaders in the development of modern literature, especially those founded for the promotion of a specific program or cause.

Ransom, John Crowe. "These Little Magazines." AMERICAN SCHOLAR, 15 (1946), 550-51.

The editor of the KENYON REVIEW presents in general terms his concept of the characteristics and function of the little magazine.

Rogers, W.G. WISE MEN FISH HERE: THE STORY OF FRANCES STELOFF AND THE GOTHAM BOOK MART. New York: Harcourt, Brace & World, 1965.

Chapter XIII (pp. 108-23) discusses the support given to little magazines by Frances Steloff. Her shop, for instance, was agent for TRANSITION; an eighth of that journal's circulation passed through the Book Mart.

Rorty, James. "Life's Delicate Children." NATION, 17 April 1929, pp. 470-71.

Rorty views a number of periodicals, including FRONTIER, POETRY, and PALMS, generally to the disparagement of the dominant New York literary scene.

Sillen, Samuel. "The Challenge of Randolph Bourne." MASSES AND MAINSTREAM, 6 (December 1953), 24-32.

This discussion of Bourne's ideas includes information on his involvement with the NEW REPUBLIC and the SEVEN ARTS.

Smith, Herbert F. "Michael Monahan and His Little Known Little Magazine." JOURNAL OF THE RUTGERS UNIVERSITY LIBRARY, 24 (December 1960), 24-28.

Monahan founded and edited the PAPYRUS from 1904 to 1914, and then the PHOENIX from 1914 to 1916, most of the time from New York City. Although little known today, he helped to introduce modern writers and rebelled from nineteenth-century literary traditions.

Steloff, Frances. "Little Magazines." JOURNAL OF MODERN LITERATURE, 4 (1975), 763-66.

The owner of the Gotham Book Mart briefly describes her promotion of various little magazines by displaying them on her shelves and taking subscriptions from customers.

Stock, Noel. THE LIFE OF EZRA POUND. New York: Random House, 1970.

Chapter XII, "THE LITTLE REVIEW, 1917/1918," covers Pound's activities as that journal's London editor, discovering new talent and sending work back to Chicago. His efforts before and after that time for POETRY and the DIAL are covered in other chapters.

Swallow, Alan. "The Little Magazines." PRAIRIE SCHOONER, 16 (1942), 238-43.

This article delineates categories of little magazines, including those which pay for contributions, those which don't, and those devoted exclusively to one literary form or another. Swallow also discusses the economics of these publications, and their literary importance. This essay also appeared in his AN EDITOR'S ESSAYS OF TWO DECADES (Seattle: Experiment Press, 1962), pp. 232-44.

______. "Postwar Little Magazines." PRAIRIE SCHOONER, 23 (1949), 152-57.

Swallow evaluates the functions of these journals and how well various of them are fulfilling those functions. This article also was published in his AN EDITOR'S ESSAYS OF TWO DECADES

(Seattle: Experiment Press, 1962), pp. 245-55.

_____. "Story of a Publisher." NEW MEXICO QUARTERLY, 36 (1966-67), 301-24.

Swallow relates his career as an independent publisher. He was poetry editor of the NEW MEXICO QUARTERLY REVIEW from 1942 to 1948 and was involved in the publication of the following little magazines: SAGE (at the University of Wyoming), MODERN VERSE, EXPERIMENT, and the ADVANCE GUARD.

_____. "Why the Little Magazines?" AN EDITOR'S ESSAYS OF TWO DECADES. Seattle: Experiment Press, 1962, pp. 256-63.

Little magazines have performed four main functions for modern literature: (1) they provide a market for the best writing not published in books, (2) they "keep the literary atmosphere stirred up," (3) they "give a hearing to the unpopular ideas," and (4) they may "provide a training ground for the writer." This essay first appeared in the October 1952 issue of AUTHOR & JOURNALIST.

Tietjens, Eunice. THE WORLD AT MY SHOULDER. New York: Macmillan, 1938.

The author relates her experiences with Harriet Monroe and poets associated with her journal in chapters II and III, "I Join POETRY: A MAGAZINE OF VERSE" and "My Friends the Poets." She discusses the founding of her friend Margaret Anderson's periodical in chapter IV, "THE LITTLE REVIEW."

Towne, Charles Hanson. "The One-Man Magazines." AMERICAN MERCURY, 63 (1946), 104-8.

Towne considers one-man journals, such as William Marion Reedy's REEDY'S MIRROR and Thomas B. Mosher's BIBELOT, to be often the most successful of literary publications.

Traver, Robert. "Where the Sound of Mimeographs?" CARLETON MISCELLANY, 6 (Winter 1965), 87-89.

During the 1930's young writers had outlets for their work in the little magazines because "when one fell two sprang up in its place and the sound of mimeographs rang in the land." With the return of prosperity these outlets disappeared.

Troy, William. "The Story of the Little Magazines." BOOKMAN, 70 (1930), 476-81, 657-63.

This brief history includes short discussions of the following journals:

The LITTLE REVIEW, the DIAL, the SEVEN ARTS, POETRY, and REEDY'S MIRROR. Troy also surveys English and "exile" little magazines.

Val Baker, Denys. LITTLE REVIEWS: 1914-1943. London: George Allen & Unwin, 1943.

Although this short study (53 pp.) focuses primarily on English periodicals, the author does discuss the LITTLE REVIEW, BROOM, and TRANSITION. In chapter VII the author turns briefly to the American literary scene in the late 1930's and concludes that "whereas, here, they were diminishing in number and quality, America was supporting new review after new review, and her older reviews were flourishing as never before."

Vivas, Eliseo. "Criticism and the Little Mags." WESTERN REVIEW, 16 (1951), 9-19.

Vivas feels that little magazines, and he includes here periodicals such as the SEWANEE, KENYON, and HUDSON reviews, have significantly influenced the direction of modern literary criticism.

Wayne, John Lakmord. "Some Little Magazines of the Past." HOBBIES: THE MAGAZINE FOR COLLECTORS, 45 (May 1940), 106-7.

This article briefly reviews the dates and policies of a number of periodicals, including SECESSION, BROOM, the FUGITIVE, and the LITTLE REVIEW.

Weaver, Mike. WILLIAM CARLOS WILLIAMS: THE AMERICAN BACKGROUND. Cambridge: At the University Press, 1971.

In "The 'Contact' Idea," Weaver discusses the contents of the journal edited by Williams and Robert McAlmon. "'Blast' and the Proletarians" covers Williams's short story contributions to a radical literary periodical edited by Fred Miller in the 1930's. "'The Lyric' and the 'red decade'" relates the attacks made on Williams and other poets by Mrs. Virginia Kent Cummins in her right-wing periodical from 1948 to 1952.

Whittemore, Reed, et al. "Foundations & Magazines: a Symposium." CARLETON MISCELLANY, 4 (Spring 1963), 45-83.

Twelve contributors, involved with either the little magazines or the foundations or both, give their views on the subsidization of periodicals. Hayden Carruth, former editor of POETRY, describes that journal's near-collapse in 1949, only prevented by a foundation grant.

Williams, William Carlos. "The Advance Guard Magazine." CONTACT, 1

(February 1932), 86-90.

"This note is just to mention a sequence of names and to comment briefly on those with which I am familiar."

______. THE SELECTED LETTERS OF WILLIAM CARLOS WILLIAMS. Ed. John C. Thirlwall. New York: McDowell, Obolensky, 1957.

Chapter II, "THE APPRENTICE POET--Imagism and the Little Magazine: 1914-1922," includes editorial explanations of Williams's activities on little magazines. He edited one issue of OTHERS, and some of the letters he wrote to poets at that time are included. Letters to Harriet Monroe, editor of POETRY, and to Kenneth Burke, contributor to OTHERS, editor of the DIAL, and a founder of SECESSION, are also included in this chapter.

Z[abel], M[orton] D[auwen]. "Recent Magazines." POETRY, 38 (1931), 170-73.

Zabel discusses the contents and policies of a number of publications, including SYMPOSIUM, HOUND & HORN, and LEFT, a new journal from Iowa which "deserves a far larger support than it is likely to find."

______. "Recent Magazines." POETRY, 41 (1933), 343-49.

The contents and policies of three new little magazines are reviewed, the NEW ACT, the LION AND CROWN, and SNAKE.

______. "Recent Magazines." POETRY, 43 (1933), 168-73.

Zabel examines the contents of current issues of HOUND & HORN, SYMPOSIUM, the WESTMINSTER MAGAZINE of Oglethorpe University in Georgia, and the WINDSOR QUARTERLY of Hartland Four Corners, Vermont. Of HOUND & HORN he says, "The note of preciosity in taste and reading begins to diminish; the threat of cult and refined isolation is less apparent," because the journal shows a growing interest in "American cultural sources and projects."

______. "The Way of Periodicals." POETRY, 34 (1929), 330-34.

After paying tribute to the DIAL and the LITTLE REVIEW, Zabel discusses in general terms the problems facing a literary periodical after the initial novelty and excitement have worn off.

## STUDIES OF INDIVIDUAL PERIODICALS

### ACCENT (1940-60)

Curley, Daniel; George Scouffas; and Charles Sattuck, eds. ACCENT: AN ANTHOLOGY, 1940-60. Urbana: University of Illinois Press, 1973.

An introduction (pp. xi-xix) traces ACCENT's history from its founding by Kerker Quinn at Bradley University, and includes information on editorial policy and on circulation and budget figures.

### THE AMERICAN SPECTATOR (1932-37)

Hagemann, E.R., and James E. Marsh. "THE AMERICAN SPECTATOR, 1932-1937: A Selected and Annotated Check-List." BULLETIN OF BIBLIOGRAPHY, 22 (1958), 132-37.

After a brief survey of the journal's history, the compilers state that their "method of selection has simply been to include contributions by writers of acknowledged reputation; on the other hand, we did feel it necessary to include poems, stories, sketches, and, finally, literary criticism of almost any type."

### APPROACH (1947-67)

"Credit Lines." APPROACH, no. 64 (Summer 1967), pp. 3-6.

This summary of APPROACH's publishing and editorial history precedes "Cumulative Index, 1947-1967" (pp. 7-31) in the same issue.

Fowler, Helen. "The APPROACH Story." APPROACH, no. 43 (Spring 1962), pp. 34-37.

This article describes the unforeseen difficulties encountered by APPROACH's founders, their solutions to these problems, and their consequent success in establishing the periodical.

### BLUES (1929-30)

Ford, Charles Henri, and Parker Tyler. "BLUES: What Happens to a Radical Literary Magazine." SEWANEE REVIEW, 39 (1931), 62-67.

Two editors of BLUES discuss the hostile reception of the publication by the more conservative literary establishment.

Williams, William Carlos. "For a New Magazine." BLUES, 1 (1929), 30-32.

Williams, a contributing editor, urges literary freedom and experimentation in BLUES, "all the extant magazines in America being thoroughly, totally, completely dead as far as anything new in literature among us is concerned."

BROOM (1921-24)

Cowley, Malcolm. EXILE'S RETURN: A LITERARY ODYSSEY OF THE 1920'S. New York: Viking Press, 1951.

"This book is the story to 1930 of what used to be called the lost generation of American writers." In chapter VI, "The City of Anger," Cowley relates his part in the struggle to keep BROOM alive. He was its associate editor from August 1923 to its death in January 1924. This material first appeared in the NEW REPUBLIC, 21 October 1931, pp. 259-62, and 11 November 1931, pp. 345-48.

Loeb, Harold. "BROOM: Beginning and Revival." CONNECTICUT REVIEW, 4, no. 4 (1970), 5-12.

The founder and editor of BROOM relates the journal's history.

______. THE WAY IT WAS. New York: Criterion Books, 1959.

Loeb was the moving force behind BROOM, from its initial conception to the journal's move to New York in 1922. In chapters I and V through XII, he relates in detail his sojourn in Paris and Berlin while publishing BROOM. He discusses his constant struggle to finance the venture, his relationships with contributors and associates, including his New York editor Lola Ridge, and the editorial goals for which he strove.

CONTACT (1920-23, 1932)

McAlmon, Robert. McALMON AND THE LOST GENERATION: A SELF-PORTRAIT. Ed. Robert E. Knoll. Lincoln: University of Nebraska Press, 1962.

"CONTACT" (pp. 140-48) includes a discussion of the philosophy behind the founding of the journal, and a letter from McAlmon to coeditor William Carlos Williams reflecting on the meaning of the journal's title.

Williams, William Carlos. "The CONTACT Story." CONTACT (San Francisco), 1, no. 1 (1959), 75-77.

Williams briefly recounts his founding with McAlmon of the first CONTACT in this first number of the San Francisco periodical of the same name. "The name typified a direct approach to life which typified many of the writers of the period and in America, at least, a concern with the local idiom." He also notes that "Hemingway's earliest short stories, before even the Paris days, would not have been possible without the CONTACT backing and my own SPRING AND ALL owes its appearance solely to CONTACT."

THE DIAL (1880-1916 in Chicago, 1916-29 in New York)

Allen, Charles. "THE DIAL." UNIVERSITY REVIEW, 10 (1943), 101-8.

Allen relates the journal's publishing and editorial history.

Cane, Melville. "The Ladies of the DIAL." AMERICAN SCHOLAR, 40 (1971), 316-21.

Cane published five poems in the DIAL in the 1920's. Here he relates the thoughtful treatment received from managing editors Alyse Gregory and Marianne Moore.

"The 'Dial's' Outlook on Literature." AMERICAN REVIEW OF REVIEWS, 41 (1910), 621.

This short article praises the DIAL and editor Francis Fisher Browne, citing his conservative view of modern literary trends: "If bankruptcy be a failure to meet just obligations, there is a good deal to be said for the view that modern literature is dangerously close to the insolvent state."

Fourier, Ruth Gasser. "The Literary Criticism of the DIAL, 1920-1929." Dissertation, Vanderbilt University, 1959.

Although the DIAL originally stated a policy of eclecticism, it eventually fostered a specific theory of literature, the result of strong influence by Ford Madox Heuffer, T.S. Eliot, and Ezra Pound.

Gregory, Alyse. THE DAY IS GONE. New York: E.P. Dutton, 1948.

Alyse Gregory succeeded Gilbert Seldes as managing editor of the Dial, and in chapter XXXI, "THE DIAL Magazine," she relates some of her experiences.

Hall, Donald. "Marianne Moore." WRITERS AT WORK: THE PARIS REVIEW INTERVIEWS. 2nd Series. New York: Viking Press, 1963, pp. 61-87.

In the course of this interview Moore talks about her work as an editor of the DIAL. The interview first appeared in the PARIS REVIEW, no. 26 (Summer-Fall 1961), pp. 41-66.

Healy, J.J. "THE DIAL and the Revolution in Poetry: 1912-1917: A Study in Controversy." BULLETIN OF THE BRITISH ASSOCIATION FOR AMERICAN STUDIES, no. 10 (June 1965), pp. 48-60.

The conservative DIAL attacked the free verse movement and POETRY: A MAGAZINE OF VERSE from 1912 until 1916, at which time C.J. Masseck, himself sympathetic to the new poetry, became editor of the journal. In YEARS OF TRANSITION: THE DIAL, 1912-1920 Nicholas Joost criticizes Healy for failing "to distinguish the basic shifts in editorial policy that occurred in the years 1913-16."

Herbst, Josephine. "Only the Best." KENYON REVIEW, 27 (1965), 353-59.

Although it is a review of Nicholas Joost's SCOFIELD THAYER AND THE DIAL: AN ILLUSTRATED HISTORY, this article presents a useful survey of the journal's history and editorial outlook.

Joost, Nicholas. "Culture vs. Power: Randolph Bourne, John Dewey, and THE DIAL." MIDWEST QUARTERLY, 9 (1968), 245-59.

Joost discusses the political views expressed in the DIAL from 1917 to 1919, while it was owned by Martyn Johnson. The journal's views of World War I were confusing and contradictory, as evidenced by the fact that "within the space of nine months, the editorial policy . . . first persecuted and drove away its most brilliant voice only to admit later that Randolph Bourne had been right after all."

______. "THE DIAL: A Journalistic Emblem and Its Tradition." In "Essays in English Literature of the Classical Period Presented to Douglas Macmillan," supp. to STUDIES IN PHILOLOGY, 64 (January 1967), 167-81.

Joost examines the philosophies of the various journals which have carried the DIAL title, and discusses their use of the title and the significance of their emblems.

______. "THE DIAL in Transition." JOURNAL OF THE ILLINOIS STATE HISTORICAL SOCIETY, 59 (1966), 272-88.

During the seven years after the death in 1913 of the DIAL's founder Francis Fisher Browne, the journal drifted uncertainly from its conservative literary views toward a support of the new movement in letters.

_____. "Ernest Hemingway and THE DIAL." NEOPHILOLOGUS, 5 (1968), 180-90, 304-13.

Joost relates in detail Hemingway's relationship with the DIAL in the 1920's, including his submissions to the journal, the circumstances of each rejection, and the resulting bitterness on the writer's part. Hemingway's sense of betrayal by Ernest Walsh, coeditor of THIS QUARTER, is also discussed, and Walsh exonerated. Joost's version of these events differs from William Wasserstrom's in "Hemingway, the DIAL, and Ernest Walsh," SOUTH ATLANTIC QUARTERLY, 65 (1966), 171-77.

_____. SCOFIELD THAYER AND THE DIAL: AN ILLUSTRATED HISTORY. Carbondale: Southern Illinois University Press, 1964.

This study concentrates on the DIAL's policies toward art and includes numerous prints from the journal. Joost examines the DIAL's publishing history beginning with the Chicago years.

_____. "Some Primitives in THE DIAL of the Twenties." FORUM, 10 (Winter 1972), 34-44; 11 (Spring 1973), 12-18.

The DIAL published much primitive and naive art and literature, especially from Southwest American Indian culture, following and partly in response to World War I. Joost discusses in detail the contents of the periodical during this time.

_____. YEARS OF TRANSITION: THE DIAL, 1912-1920: AN ILLUSTRATED HISTORY. Barre, Mass.: Barre Publishers, 1967.

This book examines in detail the changes in policy, editors, and publishers that occurred during this period. The DIAL, which under Francis Fisher Browne was liberal in its social views but conservative in its aesthetic views, became, by the time it had been moved from Chicago to New York, an advocate of the new movement in poetry. Joost discusses the careers of men connected with the journal, including Randolph Bourne and Scofield Thayer, and the history of other literary periodicals related to the DIAL's development, including the CHAP-BOOK, ART, and the TRIMMED LAMP.

Joost, Nicholas, and Alvin Sullivan. D.H. LAWRENCE AND THE DIAL. Carbondale: Southern Illinois University Press, 1970.

Lawrence's contributions throughout the 1920's, including fiction, nonfiction, and poetry, are thoroughly discussed, as well as his relations with the journal's editors. In addition, chapter VIII covers "Reviews and Advertisements in THE DIAL: A Summary." Appendix A lists the "Contributions, Reviews, Advertisements," and appendix B notes those parts of SEA AND SARDINIA published in the DIAL.

______, comps. THE DIAL, TWO AUTHOR INDEXES: ANONYMOUS & PSEUDONYMOUS CONTRIBUTORS; CONTRIBUTORS IN CLIPSHEETS. Edwardsville: Southern Illinois University Libraries, 1971.

"Our decision has been to supplement the original indexes to the DIAL (and their reprint edition as well) with a cumulative index to all the anonymous and pseudonymous contributions that we have been able to trace."

McAndrew, John. "The DIAL Collection." SATURDAY REVIEW, 27 June 1959, pp. 27-28.

In discussing an exhibition of art works which were reproduced in the DIAL's pages, McAndrews comments on Scofield Thayer's knowledge of art and his use of this material in his journal.

Moore, Marianne. "THE DIAL." LIFE AND LETTERS TODAY, 27 (1940), 175-83; 28 (1941), 3-9.

One of the DIAL's editors recalls personal experiences, letters from contributors, and policies of the periodical.

______. "THE DIAL: A Retrospect." PARTISAN REVIEW, 9 (1942), 52-58.

Moore remembers the literary accomplishments of the DIAL and the personalities associated with it. This essay was also published in PREDILECTIONS (New York: Viking Press, 1955), pp. 103-14.

Munson, Gorham B. "Expose No. 1." SECESSION, no. 1 (Spring 1922), pp. 22-24.

Munson criticizes the DIAL's editorial policies, especially the choice of Sherwood Anderson for the 1921 DIAL Award: "It would be less compromising to go one way or the other. Stay on dry land like the ATLANTIC MONTHLY or leap headfirst into the contemporary stream."

Reutlinger, Dagmar. "E.E. Cummings and the DIAL Collection." MASSACHUSETTS REVIEW, 16 (1975), 353-56.

Cummings's close relationship to the DIAL is discussed, with the focus on the art work he published in the journal.

Stearns, Harold E. THE STREET I KNOW. New York: Lee Furman, 1935.

Stearns edited the DIAL during the months just before and after its move to New York in 1918. In chapter IX, "The DIAL under a Dark Sky," he describes the social and political atmosphere in which THE DIAL was published--an atmosphere created by the war. Nicholas Joost considers this account to be somewhat unreliable.

See Nicholas Joost, "Culture vs. Power: Randolph Bourne, John Dewey, and THE DIAL," cited above.

Wasserstrom, William. "Hemingway, the DIAL, and Ernest Walsh." SOUTH ATLANTIC QUARTERLY, 65 (1966), 171-77.

Wasserstrom contends that Hemingway purposefully and maliciously associated Walsh with the DIAL in "The Man Who Was Marked for Death," a chapter in A MOVEABLE FEAST (see the General Studies section of this chapter, above). Walsh was an editor of THIS QUARTER, and had nothing to do with the DIAL. For a different version see Nicholas Joost, "Ernest Hemingway and THE DIAL," cited above.

______. "Marianne Moore, THE DIAL, and Kenneth Burke." WESTERN HUMANITIES REVIEW, 17 (1963), 249-62.

This article covers Moore's editorship of the DIAL from 1925 to 1929, Burke's close association with the journal, and the relationship of their outlooks on literature and society to the viewpoints of Scofield Thayer and James Sibley Watson, Jr., publishers of the periodical.

______. THE TIME OF THE DIAL. Syracuse, N.Y.: Syracuse University Press, 1963.

Wasserstrom exhaustively covers the editing and publishing history of the DIAL, providing information on the editors, writers, and artists associated with the journal. This study also contains useful information on a number of other literary periodicals, among them POETRY, the SEVEN ARTS, the YALE REVIEW, and HOUND & HORN.

______. "T.S. Eliot and THE DIAL." SEWANEE REVIEW, 70 (1962), 81-92.

Eliot's association with the DIAL is examined. Most notably, he published "The Waste Land" there and received the DIAL Award in 1922. Wasserstrom concludes, "THE DIAL's crusade in Eliot's behalf is identical in spirit with Thayer's crusade in behalf of American letters."

______, ed. A DIAL MISCELLANY. Syracuse, N.Y.: Syracuse University Press, 1963.

In his introduction Wasserstrom reviews the DIAL's policies and publishing history.

Zingman, Barbara Gold. "An Index to THE DIAL: 1920-1929." Dissertation, University of Louisville, 1971.

The authors and titles of all signed contributions are included, as well as those of 1,200 previously anonymous book reviews published from 1925 to 1929. An introductory chapter analyzes the bibliographical information and discusses the DIAL's history and influence.

FIRE (1926)

Hughes, Langston. "Harlem Literati in the Twenties." SATURDAY REVIEW OF LITERATURE, 22 June 1940, pp. 13-14.

Hughes relates the founding of FIRE in 1926 by a group of black artists and writers. The journal cost too much to print and lasted only one issue.

THE FUGITIVE (1922-25)

Allen, Charles. "THE FUGITIVE." SOUTH ATLANTIC QUARTERLY, 43 (1944), 382-89.

Allen traces the journal's history from the date of its founding by a group of writers in Nashville, Tennessee. This poetry journal was not founded to promote a regional philosophy, although some of its writers later led the agrarian movement.

Bradbury, John M. THE FUGITIVES: A CRITICAL ACCOUNT. Chapel Hill: University of North Carolina Press, 1958.

Chapter II, "THE FUGITIVE," focuses on the different theories of poetry expressed by John Crowe Ransom, Allen Tate, and Donald Davidson in the journal. Bradbury concludes that "the enthusiastic unanimity of its beginning had been dissipated, but the cofraternity of its editors had never been broken. Ideologically and artistically they were taking different directions, asserting individualities which generally had been submerged in the group effect."

Cowan, Louise. THE FUGITIVE GROUP: A LITERARY HISTORY. Baton Rouge: Louisiana State University Press, 1959.

Chapter III is entitled "The Birth of THE FUGITIVE: Spring, 1922," and chapter VII, "The End of THE FUGITIVE: 1925." These chapters, and the three in between, present a close analysis of the journal's poetic content and editorial outlook. An appendix (pp. 258-67) lists the contents of the FUGITIVE for each issue.

Davidson, Donald. "The Thankless Muse and the Fugitive Poets." SEWANEE REVIEW, 66 (1958), 201-28.

Davidson explains the poetic philosophy of the group for which the

FUGITIVE was the mouthpiece. He discusses the meetings in which selections for the journal were made, as well as the reasons for the cessation of publication in 1925.

Davidson, Donald, and Allen Tate. THE LITERARY CORRESPONDENCE OF DONALD DAVIDSON AND ALLEN TATE. Ed. John Tyree Fain and Thomas Daniel Young. Athens: University of Georgia Press, 1974.

Part 1 includes letters written during the "Years of THE FUGITIVE: 1922-1925," some of which discuss the politics of the journal's publication.

Holman, C. Hugh. "Literature and Culture: The FUGITIVE-Agrarians." SOCIAL FORCES, 37 (1958), 15-19.

In studying this literary group as an example of "certain significant aspects of the relationship of the artist to his culture," Holman presents the editorial outlook of their journal.

Peterson, Clell T. "The Fugitives and THE FUGITIVE." AMERICAN BOOK COLLECTOR, 10 (May 1960), 7-10.

A brief review of the journal's history is followed by facsimiles of some of its pages.

Squires, Radcliffe. ALLEN TATE: A LITERARY BIOGRAPHY. New York: Pegasus, 1971.

Chapter II, "The Fugitives," relates the history of the FUGITIVE, focusing on the development of Tate as a poet. Squires concludes by stating that "Warren would take to THE SOUTHERN REVIEW; Ransom to THE KENYON REVIEW; and Tate to THE SEWANEE REVIEW. In this way THE FUGITIVE rose from its ashes to continue in the most powerful and sensitive voices in American culture for a span of three decades."

Stewart, John L. THE BURDEN OF TIME: THE FUGITIVES AND AGRARIANS, THE NASHVILLE GROUPS OF THE 1920'S AND 1930'S, AND THE WRITING OF JOHN CROWE RANSOM, ALLEN TATE, AND ROBERT PENN WARREN. Princeton, N.J.: Princeton University Press, 1965.

The first two chapters of this detailed account, "The Fugitives: Beginnings" and "The Fugitive Group: 1922-1928," include the history of the journal. The decision finally to cease publication, and the reasons leading to it, are covered in detail. Includes an index for specific page references.

Tate, Allen. "THE FUGITIVE 1922-1925: A Personal Recollection Twenty Years After." PRINCETON UNIVERSITY LIBRARY CHRONICLE, 3 (1941), 75-84.

Tate recalls the history of the FUGITIVE, including the private poetry meetings in Nashville which led to the journal's founding. He discusses the roles that Dr. Sidney M. Hirsch, John Crowe Ransom, and Donald Davidson, among others, played in the journal's development. This essay also appears in Tate's MEMOIRS AND OPINIONS, 1926-1974 (Chicago: Swallow Press, 1975), pp. 24-34.

Young, Thomas Daniel, and M. Thomas Inge. DONALD DAVIDSON. New York: Twayne, 1971.

"Fugitive Days" (pp. 36-40) demonstrates that "Davidson's associations with the Fugitive group and his experiences with THE FUGITIVE are among the most important and influential upon his development as man and artist."

FURIOSO (1939-53)

Whittemore, Reed. "A Brief History of a Little Magazine, and Other Matters." THE BOY FROM IOWA: POEMS AND ESSAYS. New York: Macmillan, 1962, pp. 92-111. Originally in NEW WORLD WRITING, no. 15 (1950), pp. 78-95.

Whittemore reflects upon his founding and editing of FURIOSO. In considering the journal's failure, he concludes, "Our various sallies into politics and science and other green fields for amateurism were tentative and uncertain, while our preoccupation with literary matters was obsessive. Thus, while our program called for criticizing literary professionalism, we constantly identified ourselves with the profession."

GYROSCOPE (1929-30)

Cunningham, J.V. "The 'Gyroscope' Group." BOOKMAN, 75 (1932), 703-8.

GYROSCOPE was founded in 1929 in Palo Alto, California, by a group of writers including Yvor Winters, Janet Lewis, and Howard Baker. It ceased publication in February of the next year.

THE HARVARD ADVOCATE (1866-current)

Culler, Jonathan D., ed. HARVARD ADVOCATE CENTENNIAL ANTHOLOGY. Cambridge, Mass.: Schenkman Publishing Co., 1966.

In an introduction (pp. xv-xxxi), Culler surveys the history of the ADVOCATE. On pages 459-60 is a list entitled "Presidents and Pegasi of the ADVOCATE, 1866-1966."

Hall, Donald. "THE HARVARD ADVOCATE." NEW YORK TIMES BOOK REVIEW, 15 May 1966, pp. 2, 42.

Hall recalls the screening process used when he became an editor of the ADVOCATE in 1948. He also depicts the highly critical yet clubbish tone of the editorial rooms.

______, ed. THE HARVARD ADVOCATE ANTHOLOGY. New York: Twayne, 1950.

"Introduction: THE HARVARD ADVOCATE: 1866-1950" traces the journal's history. Hall focuses on the verse of T.S. Eliot and Conrad Aiken which appeared in the ADVOCATE and on the occasional conflicts which occurred between the editors and the administration or Cambridge authorities. "The Origin of the ADVOCATE" (pp. 27-33) includes two editorials from the first issue in May 1866, both of which criticize the suppression of the weekly COLLEGIAN, the periodical which the ADVOCATE succeeded.

HOUND & HORN (1927-34)

Greenbaum, Leonard. "THE HOUND AND HORN: Episodes in American Literary History, 1927-1934." Dissertation, University of Michigan, 1963.

______. THE HOUND & HORN: THE HISTORY OF A LITERARY QUARTERLY. The Hague: Mouton, 1966.

This book examines in detail the literary and social views of the journal. The HOUND & HORN embraced three major movements that arose during its seven-year career--humanism, agrarianism, and Marxism. Chapter XI, "The Critical Reception," covers the response to the HOUND & HORN by other literary periodicals.

______. "The HOUND & HORN Archive." YALE UNIVERSITY LIBRARY GAZETTE, 39 (1965), 137-46.

Greenbaum traces the history of the journal through its "dalliance with Humanism, then the association with Pound-ism, followed in order by Agrarianism, Winters-ism, Marxism, and James-ism." Using the private letters and files of the periodical in the Beinecke Rare Book and Manuscript Library at Yale, Greenbaum is able to reconstruct the alliances and conflicts that resulted in these changes of allegiance.

Kirstein, Lincoln. "The HOUND & HORN, 1927-1934." HARVARD ADVOCATE, 121 (Christmas 1934), 6-10, 92-94.

Kirstein relates his intentions and experiences as editor of the journal.

THE LITTLE REVIEW (1914-29)

Allen, Charles [A.]. "American Little Magazines--THE LITTLE REVIEW." AMERICAN PREFACES, 3 (1938), 54-59.

Allen relates the journal's editorial history.

Anderson, Margaret. MY THIRTY YEARS' WAR. New York: Covici, Friede, 1930.

The author recounts her experiences editing the LITTLE REVIEW with her partner Jane Heap, including the trial resulting from the serial publication of James Joyce's ULYSSES in the journal.

_____. "'Ulysses' in Court." LITTLE REVIEW, 7 (January-March 1921), 22-25.

The LITTLE REVIEW editor briefly relates her observations of and feelings about the ULYSSES trial, specifically her sense that the entire court proceeding was a farce.

_____, ed. THE LITTLE REVIEW ANTHOLOGY. New York: Hermitage House, 1953.

Margaret Anderson presents what she feels is the best of the REVIEW's contents. Also included at the end is the final issue of the LITTLE REVIEW and a letter from T.S. Eliot regretting the publication's demise.

Bryer, Jackson R[obert]. "Joyce, ULYSSES, and the LITTLE REVIEW." SOUTH ATLANTIC QUARTERLY, 66 (1967), 148-64.

Bryer examines the publication of various chapters of ULYSSES in the LITTLE REVIEW, Ezra Pound's role as the communicating link between Joyce and the editors, and lawyer John Quinn's defense of ULYSSES in the 1921 obscenity trial. This version of the trial differs somewhat from Nicholas Joost's, as Joost notes in YEARS OF TRANSITION: THE DIAL, 1912-1920 (Barre, Mass.: Barre Publishers, 1967), page 30, footnote 2.

_____. "'A Trial-Track for Racers': Margaret Anderson and the LITTLE REVIEW." Dissertation, University of Wisconsin, 1965.

Bryer relates the history of the journal and analyzes its contents.

Johnson, Abby Ann Arthur. "The Personal Magazine: Margaret C. Anderson and the LITTLE REVIEW, 1914-1929." SOUTH ATLANTIC QUARTERLY, 75 (1976), 351-63.

This article examines Margaret Anderson's role in the history of the journal and concludes that "The LITTLE REVIEW represents the best that was in Margaret Anderson. In so doing, it illustrates the possibilities, and also the problems, of the personal magazine."

Lohf, Kenneth A., and Eugene P. Sheehy. "Why Index THE LITTLE REVIEW?" BULLETIN OF THE NEW YORK PUBLIC LIBRARY, 66 (1962), 101-3.

This short sketch of the journal's history is an excerpt from the introduction to the INDEX (see next entry).

______, comps. AN INDEX TO THE LITTLE REVIEW 1914-1929. New York: New York Public Library, 1961.

Todd, Ruthven. "THE LITTLE REVIEW." TWENTIETH CENTURY VERSE, no. 15-16 (February 1939), pp. 159-62.

This article discusses the journal's policies before Ezra Pound became foreign editor in May 1917, an event that Todd feels improved the REVIEW's quality immensely. "THE LITTLE REVIEW was at that time . . . a scrappy repository for anything that happened to appeal to Margaret Anderson, showing neither editorial standards nor a balanced point of view."

## MANUSCRIPTS (1934-36)

Rood, John. "Extract from an autobiography. . . ." CARLETON MISCELLANY, 6 (Winter 1965), 82-86.

Rood, with his wife Mary Lawhead and Flola Shepard, founded, printed, and edited MANUSCRIPTS. Among the stories he published were Eudora Welty's "Death of a Salesman," accepted by MANUSCRIPTS at a time when she had almost given up writing, and Thomas Lanier (later Tennessee) Williams's "Twenty Wagon-Loads of Cotton."

## OTHERS (1915-19)

Munson, Gorham B. "The OTHERS Parade." GUARDIAN, 1 (1925), 228-34.

This article reviews the history of OTHERS from its founding to William Carlos Williams's protest against poetry magazines in the last issue, which the poet himself edited. Munson discusses the wide variety of poetry, both in terms of form and quality, which appeared in OTHERS.

## PAGANY (1929-32)

Halpert, Stephen, and Richard Johns. A RETURN TO PAGANY: THE HISTORY, CORRESPONDENCE, AND SELECTIONS FROM A LITTLE MAGAZINE, 1929-1932. Boston: Beacon Press, 1969.

In an introduction Kenneth Rexroth states that "PAGANY's lifetime spanned the breakdown of the international avant garde as the world economic crisis shut down and a quite different kind of literature emerged." This volume reprints contents from each issue of the journal and carefully traces editor Richard Johns's struggle to keep the publication alive. Correspondence between Johns and friends and contributors is also reproduced. Included is Ezra Pound's "The First Year of 'Pagany' and the Possibility of Criteria" (pp. 232-39) from the first issue of volume II, and a review (pp. 425-30) of various little magazines by Dudley Fitts which appeared in HOUND & HORN.

## PALMS (1923-30)

Watkins, Sue. "PALMS from Mexico: The Story of a Little Magazine." TEXAS QUARTERLY, 6 (Spring 1963), 73-79.

Idella Parnell founded this poetry journal in Guadalajara in 1923 and moved it to Aberdeen, Washington, in 1927. Among her contributors was D.H. Lawrence, with whom she became personally acquainted.

## THE PHILISTINE (1895-1915)

Balch, David Arnold. ELBERT HUBBARD, GENIUS OF ROYCROFT. New York: Frederick A. Stokes, 1940.

Chapter V, "THE PHILISTINE," describes Hubbard's founding of the journal, primarily as a medium of revenge and satire against his literary foes. The later chapters relate his activities as editor and, after 1900, sole contributor, until his death in 1915, including his friendship with Stephen Crane and his feuds with Jack London and Richard LeGallienne. Chapter VIII, "The Art of Making Enemies," relates Hubbard's unsuccessful attempt to found a little magazine called the FRA in 1908.

Champney, Freeman. ART AND GLORY: THE STORY OF ELBERT HUBBARD. New York: Crown, 1968.

In the course of his study Champney discusses Hubbard's work as editor of the PHILISTINE.

## POETRY: A MAGAZINE OF VERSE (1912-current)

Allen, Charles [A.]. "American Little Magazines--POETRY: A MAGAZINE OF VERSE." AMERICAN PREFACES, 3 (1937), 28-32.

Allen evaluates Harriet Monroe's contribution to modern poetry through her promotion of the imagists and other groups in the early years of POETRY. He contrasts POETRY's contents with the vapid literature of the "quality" journals, the ATLANTIC, SCRIBNER'S, and HARPER'S.

Cahill, Daniel J. HARRIET MONROE. New York: Twayne, 1973.

Chapters II and III, "The Founding of POETRY" and "POETRY: A MAGAZINE OF VERSE," relate the journal's history. Cahill focuses on Monroe's initial efforts to start POETRY, her close relationship with Ezra Pound, who helped by providing contributions from established English poets, and her conservative taste, which became more obvious in the late 1920's and early 1930's. Chapter V, "The Closing Years," includes information on her search for a successor to the editorial chair.

Cone, Eddie Gay. "The Free-Verse Controversy in American Magazines: 1912-1922." Dissertation, Duke University, 1971.

In the early years POETRY was the main voice defending and promoting free verse.

Cunningham, J.V. "Envoi." HOUND & HORN, 6 (1932), 124-30.

In this critical history and prediction of POETRY's demise, Cunningham states that the journal declined in quality from 1922 to 1929, when Marion Strobel and Jessica Nelson North were associate editors under Harriet Monroe. Monroe replies (6 [1933], 320-22) that his facts are wrong, that he overestimates the importance of subeditors, and that he is biased for the group of writers associated with GYROSCOPE. Cunningham responds that Miss Monroe is thin-skinned (6 [1933], 507-8).

Gregory, Horace. "The 'Unheard of Adventure': Harriet Monroe and POETRY." AMERICAN SCHOLAR, 6 (1937), 195-200.

Gregory examines Harriet Monroe's reasons for founding POETRY and then evaluates its importance to the culture of the Midwest and the nation.

Hansen, Harry. "Harriet Monroe, Priestess of Poetry." MIDWEST PORTRAITS: A BOOK OF MEMORIES AND FRIENDSHIPS. New York: Harcourt, Brace, 1923, pp. 253-61.

The founding of POETRY and Harriet Monroe's contribution to the development of modern poetry are discussed.

Jackson, Mabel Ella. "A Critical Analysis of POETRY: A MAGAZINE OF VERSE 1912-1922." Dissertation, University of Pittsburgh, 1971.

The journal's pioneering efforts in modern poetry are examined.

Monroe, Harriet. "Looking Backward." POETRY, 33 (1928), 32-38.

Monroe sketches briefly the "oscillations" of POETRY's editorial policies during its sixteen-year history.

_____. A POET'S LIFE: SEVENTY YEARS IN A CHANGING WORLD. New York: Macmillan, 1938.

Chapters XXV through XXXIII (pp. 251-428) present a detailed history of POETRY's first ten years. Morton Dauwen Zabel, her successor to the editorial chair upon her death in 1936, provides chapter XXXIV, "The Last Fifteen Years: 1922-1936," an account of Harriet Monroe's life and the further history of her journal. This book provides the most complete account available of the policies of POETRY and the literary figures with whom its editor came in contact.

_____. "These Five Years." POETRY, 11 (1917), 33-41.

POETRY's editor reviews the founding of the journal, including financial arrangements and editorial goals.

"Poetry and Miss Monroe." SATURDAY REVIEW OF LITERATURE, 30 July 1932, pp. 13, 17.

This article calls for a $5,000 subsidy to keep POETRY alive. A letter sent by Mary Whiteley entitled "Shall We Let It Die?" (p. 19) makes the same plea, reviewing the journal's accomplishments.

Williams, Ellen. "Harriet Monroe and the Poetry Renaissance--The First Ten Years of POETRY: A MAGAZINE OF VERSE, 1912-1922." Dissertation, University of Chicago, 1970.

Wright, Elizabeth, comp. INDEX TO FIFTY YEARS OF POETRY, A MAGAZINE OF VERSE, VOLUMES 1-100, 1912-1962. New York: AMS Reprint Co., 1963.

"The index is arranged chronologically. . . . Under the name of the author are arranged the poems, articles, books reviewed, and reviews he has contributed to POETRY Magazine."

## QUARTERLY REVIEW OF LITERATURE (1943-current)

Weiss, T[heodore], and Renee Weiss. QUARTERLY REVIEW OF LITERATURE: 30TH ANNIVERSARY POETRY RETROSPECTIVE, 19, nos. 1-2 (1974), entire issues.

The introduction to this anthology, "In Retrospect," sketches the founding, history, and editorial policies of the journal. A major change occurred in 1949, when the QUARTERLY REVIEW became primarily a publication of creative writing instead of criticism. Numbers 3 and 4 of volume 19 of the journal comprise a 30TH ANNIVERSARY PROSE RETROSPECTIVE.

## REEDY'S MIRROR (1893-1920)

Burgess, Charles E. "The Master and the MIRROR." PAPERS ON LANGUAGE & LITERATURE, 7 (1971), 382-405.

"One finds in surveying the MIRROR's references to [Henry] James and his works, from first to last, an emphasis on his obscure style and supple snobbishness, plus jibes at his expatriation. . . . Reedy was influential in his day. The weight of his own and his contributors' opinions had at least something to do with James' long eclipse from favor."

Flanagan, John T. "Reedy of the MIRROR." MISSOURI HISTORICAL REVIEW, 43 (1949), 128-44.

Flanagan focuses on political views expressed in the MIRROR. He does, however, include an editorial statement of purpose from the December 16, 1894, issue, and an attack by Reedy on Benjamin Orange Flower's reform periodical the ARENA.

Putzel, Max. "American Verse in REEDY'S MIRROR." Dissertation, Yale University, 1958.

_____. "Dreiser, Reedy, and 'DeMaupassant, Junior.'" AMERICAN LITERATURE, 33 (1962), 466-84.

This article examines Reedy's encouragement of Theodore Dreiser and Harris Merton Lyon. "Dreiser followed that weekly for the twenty-seven years Reedy edited it, regularly sought his support for books and causes, and never ceased to admire his old friend."

_____. THE MAN IN THE MIRROR: WILLIAM MARION REEDY AND HIS MAGAZINE. Cambridge, Mass.: Harvard University Press, 1963.

Putzel examines the history of the MIRROR, including Reedy's publication of the SPOON RIVER ANTHOLOGY, his interest in imagist poetry, and his relationship with Theodore Dreiser. Editor Reedy was a mediator, "one of a minute yet potent splinter group of critics who bridged the chasm between pre-Raphaelites and moderns, between Pater and Ezra Pound."

______. "Masters's 'Maltravers': Ernest McGaffey." AMERICAN LITERATURE, 31 (1960), 491-93.

Putzel identifies "Maltravers" from Masters's ACROSS SPOON RIVER as Ernest McGaffey. McGaffey introduced Masters to William Marion Reedy and directed the poet's attention to the MIRROR.

Winkler, Jean. "William Marion Reedy and the MIRROR." SAINT LOUIS REVIEW, 11 February 1933, pp. 7-10.

SECESSION (1922-24)

Allen, Charles A. "Director Munson's SECESSION." UNIVERSITY REVIEW, 5 (1938), 95-102.

This article relates the history of SECESSION, a little magazine which "was a rallying ground for 'abstractness,' 'originality,' and 'form,'" as opposed to naturalism. Allen tells of Gorham Munson's feud and fistfight with coeditor Matthew Josephson.

Munson, Gorham. "The Fledgling Years, 1916-1924." SEWANEE REVIEW, 40 (1932), 24-54.

Munson relates in detail his founding and editing of SECESSION, and describes his break with Matthew Josephson and Malcolm Cowley, both of whom later became involved with BROOM.

THE SEVEN ARTS (1916-17)

Allen, Charles [A.]. "American Little Magazines--THE SEVEN ARTS." AMERICAN PREFACES, 3 (1938), 94-96.

Allen relates the journal's publishing and editorial history.

Frank, Waldo. MEMOIRS OF WALDO FRANK. Ed. Alan Trachtenberg. Amherst: University of Massachusetts Press, 1973.

In chapter IV of part 1, "The Tragedy of the SEVEN ARTS," Frank relates his experiences as associate editor. He concludes that the editors', including his own, inability to compromise caused the death of the publication. In chapter V of part 3,

"The Magazine," Frank recalls a meeting with Reinhold Niebuhr and Lewis Mumford prior to World War II, in which plans were made for another journal, which was never founded.

Oppenheim, James. "The Story of the SEVEN ARTS." AMERICAN MERCURY, 20 (1930), 156-65.

Oppenheim discusses his founding and editing of the SEVEN ARTS. He explains the journal's loss of subsidy as a result of public reaction to articles by Randolph Bourne opposing the entry of the United States into World War I.

Ramsey, Warren. "Exiles and THE SEVEN ARTS Group: An American Dialogue." PROCEEDINGS OF THE IVTH CONGRESS OF THE INTERNATIONAL COMPARATIVE LITERATURE ASSOCIATION. Fribourg, 1964. The Hague: Mouton, 1966. I, 237-44.

Ramsey discusses the debate surrounding the SEVEN ARTS' editorial policy supporting a national literature.

Sacks, Claire. "The SEVEN ARTS Critics: A Study of Cultural Nationalism in America, 1910-1930." Dissertation, University of Wisconsin, 1955.

This study examines the cultural nationalism of Randolph Bourne, Van Wyck Brooks, Waldo Frank, and Lewis Mumford.

Silet, Charles L[oring] P[rovine]. "A Check-list of THE SEVEN ARTS." SERIF, 9 (Summer 1972), 15-21.

"The check-list contains anonymous as well as pseudonymous pieces, editorials and book reviews, short notices and featured articles. In short, it catalogues the whole magazine."

______. "THE SEVEN ARTS: The Artist and the Community." Dissertation, Indiana University, 1973.

An examination of the contents and history of the journal reveals the aspirations and frustrations experienced by the intellectual community during World War I.

Untermeyer, Louis. BYGONES: THE RECOLLECTIONS OF LOUIS UNTERMEYER. New York: Harcourt, Brace & World, 1965.

In chapter VII, "THE SEVEN ARTS," Untermeyer recalls his activities on the short-lived journal and explains the causes of its death.

## SOIL (1916-17)

Munson, Gorham. "The Skyscraper Primitives." GUARDIAN, 1 (1925), 164-78.

> SOIL, founded and edited by Robert Coady, is seen as the precursor to BROOM and other literary developments in the 1920's. Coady searched for an art that was indigenous to American life, an art found in skyscrapers, football, and popular music, distinct from the culture of Europe, and more vital.

## STORY (1931-48, 1960-63)

Burnett, Whit. THE LITERARY LIFE AND THE HELL WITH IT. New York: Harper and Brothers, 1938.

> In "The First Five Years" (pp. 107-24) Burnett humorously discusses his problems while editing STORY, first in Vienna, where he began by mimeographing it, then in Majorca, where the type was laboriously set by hand, and finally in New York.

Burnett, Whit, and Hallie Burnett, eds. STORY: THE FICTION OF THE FORTIES. New York: E.P. Dutton, 1949.

> In the foreword to this anthology (pp. xiii-xviii), the editors discuss the type of fiction which appeared in STORY and their literary discoveries, including Norman Mailer and Truman Capote.

Thorp, Willard. "Whit Burnett and STORY Magazine." PRINCETON UNIVERSITY LIBRARY CHRONICLE, 27 (1966), 107-12.

> During his editorship of STORY from 1931 to 1948, first with Martha Foley and then Hallie Burnett, Whit Burnett introduced to the public a number of writers who later became well known, including Richard Wright and Joseph Heller. Thorp presents some of the information contained in private letters and files of the journal in the Burnett papers held by the Princeton University Library.

## TRANSITION (1927-38)

Allen, Charles [A.]. "American Little Magazines: TRANSITION." AMERICAN PREFACES, 4 (1939), 115-18, 125-28.

> Allen focuses on the philosophy held by Eugene Jolas, founder and editor of TRANSITION. This philosophy, vertigralism or Transitionism, is exemplified in James Joyce's FINNEGAN'S WAKE, parts of which were first published in TRANSITION under the title "Work in Progress."

Fox, Hugh. "Eugene Jolas and TRANSITION: The Mantic Power of the Word." WEST COAST REVIEW, 7 (June 1972), 3-5.

> This article explains Jolas's theory of literature as it was expressed in TRANSITION.

Gilbert, Stuart. "Five Years of TRANSITION." TRANSITION, no. 22 (February 1933), pp. 138-43.

> Gilbert praises Jolas for fostering experimental literature, and explains that he was "the first to bring to the notice of the Anglo-American public the work of the *surrealistes*--whom America and England seem now to be '*discovering*'; some ten years late, as usual!--and to give illustrations of their texts."

Jolas, Eugene. "Ten Years Transition." PLASTIQUE, 3 (1938), 23-26.

______. "TRANSITION: An Epilogue." AMERICAN MERCURY, 23 (1931), 185-92.

> One year after TRANSITION ceased publication, Jolas gives his views of the venture in the face of what he considers unfair criticism. He points out that although he sought the work of the surrealists, he was not a surrealist himself, and after the first year he broke with them.

Jolas, Eugene, and Elliot Paul. "A Review." TRANSITION, no. 12 (March 1928), pp. 139-47.

> At the end of the first year of publication, the editors review their policies, goals, and accomplishments. They defend the international focus of their journal and criticize the narrow complacency of American critics and periodicals.

Kirstein, Lincoln. "TRANSITION." HOUND & HORN, 2 (1929), 197-98.

> Kirstein reviews TRANSITION now that it has become a quarterly. He feels that it is more valuable as a "state of mind" than for its artistry: "Unwieldy, non-selective, printing much that has little or no value, and very little that can have any claims to permanence, it is nevertheless an invaluable organ."

McMillan, Douglas [Dougald McMillan] III. "TRANSITION: A Critical and Historical Account." Dissertation, Northwestern University, 1969.

______. *TRANSITION: THE HISTORY OF A LITERARY ERA, 1927-1938.* New York: Braziller, 1976. First published London: Calder and Boyars, 1975.

> McMillan examines in detail the publishing and editorial history of TRANSITION, including information on aspects such as distribution

and printing. He also studies the career of editor Eugene Jolas, and discusses the literary figures associated with the journal. Appendix I reprints the tables of contents of the twenty-seven issues of TRANSITION.

"TRANSITION." HOUND & HORN, 1 (1927), 72-73.

This short review discusses the contents of TRANSITION's first few numbers and states that "of all the new developments in periodicals it seems worthy of most attention."

TWICE A YEAR (1938-48)

Wasserstrom, William, ed. CIVIL LIBERTIES AND THE ARTS: SELECTIONS FROM TWICE A YEAR, 1938-48. Syracuse, N.Y.: Syracuse University Press, 1964.

In the introduction to this anthology, Wasserstrom reviews TWICE A YEAR's history, focusing on the policies of its editor Dorothy Newman. He concludes: "From 1902 to 1948, from the birth of CAMERA WORK to the short-lived SEVEN ARTS, through the ripening life of THE DIAL and the intermittent life of AMERICAN CARAVAN, then finally in the troubled life of TWICE A YEAR, a vital idea in American literary journalism flourished and ended. . . . With the final number of TWICE A YEAR, Whitmanesque utopians of the 1930's lost the last organ to represent their cause."

WAVE (1922-23)

Starrett, Vincent. BORN IN A BOOKSHOP: CHAPTERS FROM THE CHICAGO RENASCENCE. Norman: University of Oklahoma Press, 1965.

In chapter XV (pp. 203-20) Starrett relates his experiences as founder and editor of WAVE, which he published in Chicago sporadically from January 1922 to June 1923.

# Chapter 5

# REGIONAL LITERARY PERIODICALS

## GENERAL STUDIES

Allen, Charles [A.]. "Regionalism and the Little Magazines." COLLEGE ENGLISH, 7 (October 1945), 10-16.

Allen examines regionalism as a literary force and mentions the MIDLAND, the NEW MEXICO QUARTERLY, and the PRAIRIE SCHOONER, among others. Paul Stewart challenges Allen's views in THE PRAIRIE SCHOONER STORY: A LITTLE MAGAZINE'S FIRST 25 YEARS (see below). Allen's article appeared almost verbatim as part of chapter VIII of THE LITTLE MAGAZINE: A HISTORY AND A BIBLIOGRAPHY (see the General Studies section of Chapter 4).

Botkin, B.A. "We Talk about Regionalism--North, East, South, and West." FRONTIER, 13 (1933), 286-96.

In discussing different types of regionalism, Botkin evaluates the editorial outlook of the FRONTIER as representative of the Northwest and the LAUGHING HORSE as representative of the Southwest.

DuBois, Arthur E. "Among the Quarterlies: This Question of 'Regionalism.'" SEWANEE REVIEW, 45 (1937), 216-27.

DuBois discusses various elements of regionalism found in the quarterlies.

"Little Magazines." INTERMOUNTAIN REVIEW, 1 (February 1937), 2.

This editorial briefly reviews the role of regional journals in the last fifteen years, and calls for subsidization of such publications either by state universities or the Federal Arts Project. In "More about Little Magazines" H.G. Merriam, editor of the FRONTIER AND MIDLAND, responds by rejecting any such subsidization (INTERMOUNTAIN REVIEW, 1 [March 1937], 2).

Peterson, Martin Severin. "Regional Magazines." PRAIRIE SCHOONER, 3 (1929), 292-95.

An associate editor of the PRAIRIE SCHOONER discusses the importance of regional magazines and briefly reviews the histories of the MIDLAND, the FRONTIER, the SOUTHWEST REVIEW, and his own journal.

Swallow, Alan. "A Magazine for the West?" AN EDITOR'S ESSAYS OF TWO DECADES. Seattle: Experiment Press, 1962, pp. 324-29.

In considering the potential for an important Western journal, Swallow speculates on the factors that made the SOUTHERN REVIEW the best and most influential literary journal in America. This essay first appeared in the Autumn 1957 issue of INLAND.

## NEW ENGLAND

### THE NEW ENGLAND QUARTERLY (1928-current)

Fry, Varian. "THE NEW ENGLAND QUARTERLY." HOUND & HORN, 1 (1928), 381-82.

Fry reviews the first two issues of the QUARTERLY, January and April 1928, and concludes that the publication appeals to the scholar and the general reader alike.

## THE SOUTH

### General Studies

Drewry, John E. "Voices of the South--National Distinction Won by Southern Literary Quarterlies (VIRGINIA QUARTERLY REVIEW, SEWANEE REVIEW, SOUTH ATLANTIC QUARTERLY, and SOUTHERN REVIEW)." CONTEMPORARY AMERICAN MAGAZINES: A SELECTED BIBLIOGRAPHY AND REPRINTS OF ARTICLES DEALING WITH VARIOUS PERIODICALS. 3rd ed. Athens: University of Georgia Press, 1938, pp. 72-76.

Drewry briefly discusses the editorial content of these periodicals.

Hobson, Fred C., Jr. SERPENT IN EDEN: H.L. MENCKEN AND THE SOUTH. Chapel Hill: University of North Carolina Press, 1974.

Chapter III, "The Little Magazines and the New Spirit," focuses on Mencken's encouragement of the New Orleans DOUBLE DEALER and the REVIEWER in the early 1920's. Other little magazines mentioned in this chapter include the PHOENIX of Emory University,

BOZART in Atlanta, and the CAROLINA MAGAZINE in Chapel Hill, all inspired by Mencken's attacks on Southern traditionalism.

Hubbell, Jay B. "Southern Magazines." CULTURE IN THE SOUTH. Ed. W.T. Couch. Chapel Hill: University of North Carolina Press, 1934, pp. 159-82.

Among the periodicals discussed are the TEXAS REVIEW (later the SOUTHWEST REVIEW), the DOUBLE DEALER, the REVIEWER, and CONTEMPO: A REVIEW OF BOOKS AND PERSONALITIES. Hubbell discusses the varying emphasis put upon regionalism by these publications.

Mencken, H[enry] L[ouis]. "The South Begins to Mutter." SMART SET, 65 (August 1921), 138-44.

Mencken, who had called the South the "Sahara of the Bozart," here recognizes the growing literary activity there, a growth accompanied by the founding of little magazines such as the DOUBLE DEALER and the REVIEWER.

## Studies of Individual Periodicals

### THE DOUBLE DEALER (1921-26)

Bowen, Frances Jean. "THE NEW ORLEANS DOUBLE DEALER: 1921-May 1926, A Critical History." Dissertation, Vanderbilt University, 1954.

This history includes a study of the journal's contents, conversations with those editors still living in New Orleans, and correspondence with sixty of the contributors.

______. "The New Orleans DOUBLE DEALER, 1921-1926." LOUISIANA HISTORICAL QUARTERLY, 39 (1956), 443-56.

Bowen relates the journal's history, from its founding by Julius Weis Friend and his associates, through its change in tone to a serious literary periodical, to its death in 1926 primarily because of financial difficulties.

Durrett, Frances Bowen. "The New Orleans DOUBLE DEALER." REALITY AND MYTH: ESSAYS IN AMERICAN LITERATURE IN MEMORY OF RICHMOND CROOM BEATTY. Ed. William E. Walker and Robert L. Welker. Nashville, Tenn.: Vanderbilt University Press, 1964, pp. 212-36.

This article includes reprints of the first published works of William Faulkner, Ernest Hemingway, and Thornton Wilder, all of which originally appeared in the DOUBLE DEALER. The policies and intentions of founders Julius Weis Friend, John McClure, and Basil Thompson are explained as well.

THE GEORGIA REVIEW (1947-current)

Eidson, John O. "THE GEORGIA REVIEW: Age Twenty." GEORGIA REVIEW, 20 (1966), 385-87.

A former editor of the GEORGIA REVIEW comments on the regional editorial outlook followed since the journal's founding.

Maloney, Stephen R. "Not for the 'Smart-Set in Omaha': The GEORGIA REVIEW and Southern Literature." NEW ORLEANS REVIEW, 4 (1974), 197-202.

THE OBSERVER (1933-34)

Knickerbocker, William S. "Asides and Soliloquies." SEWANEE REVIEW, 42 (1934), 385-90.

Knickerbocker discusses the OBSERVER, a literary journal of Memphis, published by a group influenced by the fugitive and agrarian movements.

PSEUDOPODIA (1936), later THE NORTH GEORGIA REVIEW (1937-41), later SOUTH TODAY (1942-45)

White, Helen, and Redding S. Sugg, eds. FROM THE MOUNTAIN: SELECTIONS FROM PSEUDOPODIA (1936), THE NORTH GEORGIA REVIEW (1937-1941), AND SOUTH TODAY (1942-1945). Memphis, Tenn.: Memphis State University Press, 1972.

The introduction (pp. xi-xxvi) relates the history of this liberal southern periodical. Founded and edited by Lillian Smith and Paula Snelling, the publication grew in circulation from 27 to almost 10,000. The editorial policy was broad, "although from the first the editors disassociated themselves from the approach to Southern affairs represented by the Agrarian writers and the SOUTHERN REVIEW."

THE REVIEWER (1921-25)

Cabell, James Branch. BETWEEN FRIENDS: LETTERS OF JAMES BRANCH CABELL AND OTHERS. Ed. Padraic Colum and Margaret Freeman Cabell. New York: Harcourt, Brace & World, 1962.

Cabell edited the October, November, and December 1921 issues of the REVIEWER. Correspondence relating to his editing activities is included on pages 233-40.

_____. LET ME LIE: BEING IN THE MAIN AN ETHNOLOGICAL ACCOUNT OF THE REMARKABLE COMMONWEALTH OF VIRGINIA AND THE MAKING OF ITS HISTORY. New York: Farrar, Straus, 1947.

"Part Nine: 'Published in Richmond, Virginia'" is a rambling reminiscence about the REVIEWER.

Carson, Betty Farley. "Richmond Renascence: The Virginia Writers' Club of the 1920's and THE REVIEWER." CABELLIAN, 2 (1970), 39-47.

This article relates the founding of the club in 1918 and the founding and editing of the journal. "Although there is divided opinion as to whether or not the Writers' Club itself was directly responsible for the founding of the magazine, there is agreement that the idea was brought up and planned at one of the club meetings or parties."

Clark, Emily. "At Random: Beginning the Second Volume." REVIEWER, 2 (1921), 37-40.

The REVIEWER's editor discusses the journal's goals, its regional qualities, and the reactions to its initial publication: "We received both scolding and petting in larger measure than we had dreamed of: and, though once or twice accused of timidity and caution in the North, were quite recently paid the subtle compliment of being called unconventional in the South."

_____. "At Random: The Facts of the Case Are These." REVIEWER, 2 (1922), 335-37.

Clark facetiously concludes that established writers must be published in the journal as "bait" for new, unknown writers, since the REVIEWER offers payment only "in fame not specie." She also replies to views on this issue expressed to her by Louis Untermeyer, James Branch Cabell, and H.L. Mencken.

_____. "At Random: Postscript." REVIEWER, 4 (1924), 405-8.

Upon retiring from her editorial position, Clark reviews the journal's difficulties and accomplishments. She thanks prominent writers for their contributions, since "it is mainly through the generosity of this group that THE REVIEWER has become a national, rather than a provincial magazine."

_____. INGENUE AMONG THE LIONS: THE LETTERS OF EMILY CLARK TO JOSEPH HERGESHEIMER. Ed. Gerald Langford. Austin: University of Texas Press, 1965.

Emily Clark wrote these letters to a contributor and supporter from 1921 to 1924. In his introduction (pp. xi-xxiv) Langford reviews the journal's history, Emily Clark's role in it, and the roles of a number of major contributors.

______. INNOCENCE ABROAD. New York: Alfred A. Knopf, 1931.

The REVIEWER's publishing and editorial history is related in chapter I, "THE REVIEWER--An Experiment in Southern Letters." Each chapter following focuses on one of the following contributors or associates of the journal: James Branch Cabell, Ellen Glasgow, Amelie Rives, Joseph Hergesheimer, H.L. Mencken, Carl Van Vechten, Ernest Boyd, Elinor Wylie, Frances Newman, Julia Peterkin, DuBose Heyward, Paul Green, and Gerald Johnson.

Duke, Maurice. "THE REVIEWER: A Bibliographical Guide to a Little Magazine." RESOURCES FOR AMERICAN LITERARY STUDY, 1 (1971), 58-103.

This is an annotated bibliography of the contents of each issue of the REVIEWER, introduced by an account of the journal's history.

THE SOUTH ATLANTIC QUARTERLY (1902-current)

Cline, John. "Thirty-Eight Years of the SOUTH ATLANTIC QUARTERLY." Dissertation, Duke University, 1940.

Hamilton, William B[askerville]. "Fifty Years of Liberalism and Learning." SOUTH ATLANTIC QUARTERLY, 51 (1952), 7-32.

Hamilton investigates in detail the contents of the SOUTH ATLANTIC QUARTERLY.

______, ed. FIFTY YEARS OF THE SOUTH ATLANTIC QUARTERLY. Durham, N.C.: Duke University Press, 1952.

In an essay introducing this selection of articles, Hamilton traces the history and discusses the contents of the journal.

Mims, Edwin. "Early Years of the SOUTH ATLANTIC QUARTERLY." SOUTH ATLANTIC QUARTERLY, 51 (1952), 33-63.

Mims, editor of the QUARTERLY from 1906 to 1909, recounts the early years of the journal's history and his own editorial activities. He emphasizes the QUARTERLY's role as a liberal force in the South.

______. "The Function of Criticism in the South." SOUTH ATLANTIC QUARTERLY, 31 (1932), 133-49.

Focusing on the first ten years of the SOUTH ATLANTIC QUARTERLY's history, Mims concludes that few people realize "just how significant this publication was in crystallizing the points of view of Southern liberals in the first years of this century." The QUARTERLY's editorial views contrast with those expressed by the Agrarian writers published in I'LL TAKE MY STAND (New York: Harper and Brothers, 1930).

"A Notable Victory for Academic Freedom." WORLD'S WORK, 7 (1904), 4284-87.

This article relates the events which followed editor John Bassett's publication of his article entitled "Stirring Up the Fires of Race Antipathy" in the QUARTERLY. A number of calls were made for Bassett's dismissal from Trinity College, but the board of trustees refused to accept his resignation by a count of eighteen to seven.

Sanders, Charles Richard. "SOUTH ATLANTIC QUARTERLY, The First Forty Years." SOUTH ATLANTIC BULLETIN, 8 (December 1942), 1, 12-13.

The QUARTERLY's history is surveyed, and a portion of the original statement of purpose, published by editor John Bassett in the first issue, is reprinted.

THE SOUTHERN REVIEW (1935-42)

Brooks, Cleanth, and Robert Penn Warren, eds. AN ANTHOLOGY OF STORIES FROM THE SOUTHERN REVIEW. Baton Rouge: Louisiana State University Press, 1953.

In an introduction Brooks and Warren relate the founding of the REVIEW, beginning with the initial proposal by President James Monroe Smith of Louisiana State University to Warren and Albert Erskine. They also briefly discuss the journal's publishing and editorial history. "A Complete List of Stories Published in the SOUTHERN REVIEW" is included at the end of the volume (pp. 432-35).

Montesi, Albert J. "Huey Long and THE SOUTHERN REVIEW." JOURNAL OF MODERN LITERATURE, 3 (1973), 63-74.

Montesi describes the connection between the efforts of Huey Long to promote Louisiana State University and the establishment of the SOUTHERN REVIEW there in 1935. Neither Long nor the administrators at the university attempted to control the journal's policies, and Montesi concludes that the financial sponsorship of the REVIEW by Long's appointees at the institution "was certainly not the shady, unsavory affair that some commentators claim for it."

______. "THE SOUTHERN REVIEW (1935-1942)." CHICAGO REVIEW, 16 (1964), 201-12.

Montesi presents the causes of the REVIEW's success, including the quality of its contents, its early support of the New Criticism and agrarianism, and the lack of high-quality literary journals at the time of its founding.

______. "THE SOUTHERN REVIEW (1935-1942): A History and Evaluation." Dissertation, Pennsylvania State University, 1955.

"R.P. Blackmur's Contributions to the SOUTHERN REVIEW." SOUTHERN REVIEW, NS 2 (1966), 244.

Blackmur's contributions, including essays, poems, and review essays, are listed.

UNCLE REMUS'S MAGAZINE (1907-8), later UNCLE REMUS'S THE HOME MAGAZINE (1908-13)

Mugleston, William F. "The Perils of Southern Publishing: A History of UNCLE REMUS'S MAGAZINE." JOURNALISM QUARTERLY, 52 (1975), 515-21, 608.

The periodical was founded by Joel Chandler Harris as a regional publication intended to promote the South and harmonious race relations. "Under the elder Harris it was largely an innocuous literary journal. His son [Julian LaRose Harris] turned it into a much more controversial organ of commentary on southern and national affairs."

THE VIRGINIA QUARTERLY REVIEW (1925-current)

Gold, William Jay. "The Cause of Good Books in the South." PUBLISHER'S WEEKLY, 137 (1940), 706-11.

The managing editor of the VIRGINIA QUARTERLY REVIEW discusses the founding and history of the journal, including the policies and routines of the editorial office.

POEMS FROM THE VIRGINIA QUARTERLY REVIEW: 1925-1967. Charlottesville: University Press of Virginia, 1969.

In a foreword to this anthology (pp. v-vi) Charlotte Kohler briefly relates the journal's policies concerning poetry.

THE VIRGINIA QUARTERLY REVIEW, A NATIONAL JOURNAL OF LITERATURE AND DISCUSSION: TWENTY-YEAR INDEX, 1925-1944. Charlottesville: Virginia Quarterly Review, 1946.

A preface (pp. iii-iv) provides a summary of the changes in editorial personnel which occurred during the REVIEW's first twenty years.

# THE MIDWEST

## General Studies

Anderson, Sherwood. "Little Magazines." INTERMOUNTAIN REVIEW, 2 (Fall 1937), 1.

> Anderson briefly relates the rise of little magazines in the Midwest, and states that he himself "could have found no place for the publication of my own stories but for these smaller magazines."

Andrews, Clarence A. A LITERARY HISTORY OF IOWA. Iowa City: University of Iowa Press, 1972.

> Chapter XIV, "Historians, Editors, and Publishers," includes discussion of the MIDLAND and of AMERICAN PREFACES, the last a literary journal published by the School of Letters of the University of Iowa from 1935 to 1943.

Flanagan, John T. "Some Middlewestern Literary Magazines." PAPERS ON LANGUAGE & LITERATURE, 3 (1967), 237-57.

> This survey includes the DIAL, the LITTLE REVIEW, POETRY, the CHICAGO REVIEW, the MIDLAND MONTHLY, the BELLMAN, and REEDY'S MIRROR. Flanagan concludes that "the Middle West has never had . . . a serious, sophisticated journal, both durable and profitable, which combined literary and intellectual qualities with a regional orientation sufficient to appeal to a national audience," such as one finds in the ATLANTIC, the YALE REVIEW, and the VIRGINIA QUARTERLY REVIEW.

Hoeltje, Herbert H. "Iowa Literary Magazines." PALIMPSEST, 11 (1930), 87-94.

> Hoeltje reviews the history of Johnson Brigham's MIDLAND MONTHLY; John T. Frederick's MIDLAND; the HUSK, published three times a year in Mt. Vernon beginning in 1922; and the TANAGER, a bimonthly journal published at Grinnell College since 1926.

## Studies of Individual Periodicals

### THE BELLMAN (1906-19)

Flanagan, John T. "Early Literary Periodicals in Minnesota." MINNESOTA HISTORY, 26 (1945), 293-311.

> The second half of this article covers the BELLMAN, a journal founded and edited by William C. Edgar in Minneapolis. When

he ended its successful career, Edgar concluded that "by hard work, business intelligence, and patience, it was possible to publish at a profit a weekly illustrated periodical of good quality."

THE FRONTIER (1920-33), later THE FRONTIER AND MIDLAND (1933-39)

Poindexter, Everett. "Financing the First Issue." FRONTIER, 5 (March 1925), 26.

The FRONTIER's financial manager briefly relates his attempts to secure paid advertising.

Whitham, Belle M. "Reminiscences of Creative Writing Class at the FRONTIER." FRONTIER, 5 (March 1925), 23-24.

A member of H.G. Merriam's creative writing section at the University of Montana in the fall of 1919 relates the founding of the MONTANAN by the class. "Before the next issue the name was changed to THE FRONTIER. . . . Montana has still aspects of the frontier, the last frontier, and the aim of the magazine has been to reflect the spirit of the state. . . ."

THE MIDLAND (1915-33)

Allen, Charles [A.]. "American Little Magazines--IV. THE MIDLAND." AMERICAN PREFACES, 3 (1938), 136-40.

Allen traces the MIDLAND's history, from its founding in Iowa City by John T. Frederick, who based it on the regionalist views of Josiah Royce, to its death in Chicago as a result of the Depression. This article was approved by Frederick.

Derleth, August W. "The Plight of the MIDLAND." COMMONWEAL, 17 February 1932, pp. 439-40.

Editor Frederick's plea for support to his subscribers in 1931 was successful, allowing him to continue publication for the time being. Derleth briefly reviews the journal's contributions to midwestern literature.

Hartley, Lois T. "THE MIDLAND." IOWA JOURNAL OF HISTORY, 47 (1949), 325-44.

The journal's history and contents are covered in detail, including its change from a regional to national outlook, the attitudes toward certain authors expressed in its book reviews, and the types of poetry and short stories published in it.

Mott, Frank Luther. "THE MIDLAND." PALIMPSEST, 43 (1962), 133-34.

Mott, associate editor of the MIDLAND during its stay in Iowa City, reviews the editorial history of the periodical and the activities of John T. Frederick.

______. TIME ENOUGH: ESSAYS IN AUTOBIOGRAPHY. Chapel Hill: University of North Carolina Press, 1962.

In chapter VIII, "The MIDLAND," Mott discusses the journal's history and editorial policies. He notes the support given to the publication by Edward J. O'Brien, editor of the yearly anthology entitled AMERICAN BEST SHORT STORIES.

______. "The Two MIDLANDS." PALIMPSEST, 44 (1963), 294-302.

This article relates the separate histories of the first MIDLAND MONTHLY, published from 1894 to 1899, and the later MIDLAND.

Reigelman, Milton [Monroe]. THE MIDLAND: A VENTURE IN LITERARY REGIONALISM. Iowa City: University of Iowa Press, 1975.

This history of the MIDLAND, based on Reigelman's dissertation (see below), includes indexes to contributors and to book reviews.

______. "A Study of THE MIDLAND Magazine: 1915-1933." Dissertation, University of Iowa, 1973.

In this history Reigelman notes that the domestic, rural focus of the MIDLAND's fiction contrasts with the lost generation literature of the same period.

THE PRAIRIE SCHOONER (1926-current)

Hamilton, Judith Y. "PRAIRIE SCHOONER Sampler: The First Four Years and a Four-Year Check." PRAIRIE SCHOONER, 40 (1967), 329-45.

This list of selected contents includes excerpts from important or typical stories, poems, and articles. Hamilton says that "this sampler may serve to answer 'What has PRAIRIE SCHOONER been like through the years?'"

Johnson, Maurice. "THE PRAIRIE SCHOONER: Ten Years." PRAIRIE SCHOONER, 11 (1937), 71-82.

One of the journal's associate editors reviews the contents of the first ten volumes, noting the subsequent accomplishments of the contributors.

Stewart, Paul Robert. "THE PRAIRIE SCHOONER: A Little Magazine's First Twenty-Five Years." Dissertation, University of Illinois, 1954.

_____. THE PRAIRIE SCHOONER STORY: A LITTLE MAGAZINE'S FIRST 25 YEARS. Lincoln: University of Nebraska Press, 1955.

This detailed study examines the periodical's publishing and editorial history. Chapter VII, "The SCHOONER and Its Contemporaries," deals with the cordial relationships between editor Lowry C. Wimberly and John T. Frederick and Harold G. Merriam, editors of the MIDLAND and the FRONTIER. An appendix lists contributors, their geographical distribution, and members of the staff from throughout the journal's history.

_____. "We Are Thirty." PRAIRIE SCHOONER, 30 (1956), 312-20.

Stewart relates the editorial history of the journal, including its change from regional to national focus in 1930. Much of this discussion deals with the economic and editorial problems of little magazines in general.

## THE UNIVERSITY REVIEW (1934-44), later THE UNIVERSITY OF KANSAS CITY REVIEW (1944-current)

Cappon, Alexander P. "Early Volume Numbers of THE UNIVERSITY REVIEW: A Bibliographical Curiosity." UNIVERSITY OF KANSAS CITY REVIEW, 36 (1970), 238-39.

Some confusion occurs with the first volume of the REVIEW (1934-35), which was called volume 4, as a continuation of the UNIVERSITY BULLETIN, a publication with which it actually had no connection. The next year's volume was then called volume 2, and consecutive numeration continued thereafter.

Decker, Clarence R., and Mary Bell Decker. A PLACE OF LIGHT: THE STORY OF A UNIVERSITY PRESIDENCY. New York: Hermitage House, 1954.

Chapter XII, entitled "Little Mag," covers the founding and editorial policies of the REVIEW. The chapter author, Mary Bell Decker, emphasizes the regional aspects of the journal and reader response to its contents.

Decker, Mary Bell. "THE UNIVERSITY OF KANSAS CITY REVIEW 1934-1953." UNIVERSITY OF KANSAS CITY REVIEW, 19 (1953), 219-28.

Mrs. Decker, whose husband founded the REVIEW, relates the periodical's editorial and publishing history. She reveals some of the reader reaction to literature and criticism published during the REVIEW's career.

## THE WEST

### General Studies

Bentley, Imogene. "Texas Literary and Educational Magazines: Their History and Educational Content." Dissertation, George Peabody College for Teachers, 1942.

Botkin, B.A. "FOLKSAY and SPACE: Their Genesis and Exodus." SOUTHWEST REVIEW, 20 (1935), 321-35.

Botkin reflects on his editorships of FOLK-SAY, an annual, from 1929 to 1932, and SPACE, a monthly, from 1934 to 1935. In both ventures he promoted Oklahoman culture and literature. He attributes their failure to public apathy toward regionalism and the domination of local writers by New York culture.

Ross, Morton L. "Alan Swallow and Modern, Western American Poetry." WESTERN AMERICAN LITERATURE, 1 (1966), 97-104.

This study includes information on Swallow's numerous contributions to Ray B. West's INTERMOUNTAIN REVIEW, and his work as poetry editor of the NEW MEXICO QUARTERLY REVIEW from 1942 to 1948.

### Studies of Individual Periodicals

#### INTERIM (1944-54)

Stevens, A. Wilber. "The Interim Years." SOUTH DAKOTA REVIEW, 6 (Autumn 1968), 40-46.

Stevens edited INTERIM in Seattle throughout its ten-year history. He discusses the writers and poets associated with it, and considers the extent to which it was a regional publication and owed its flavor and identity to the Northwest.

#### THE INTERMOUNTAIN REVIEW (1936-38), later THE ROCKY MOUNTAIN REVIEW (1938-46), later WESTERN REVIEW (1946-current)

Freedman, Ralph. "The Quarterly Revisited." WESTERN REVIEW, 22 (1957), 82.

Freedman argues with Granville Hicks's criticism that literary reviews are too cautious and conservative (NEW LEADER, 9 December 1957, pp. 9-10). Among other points, Freedman states that "WESTERN REVIEW has focused attention on precisely those writers whose absence from the literary journals Mr. Hicks deplores."

Stegner, Wallace, et al. "Twenty Years of WESTERN REVIEW: A Series of Recollections." WESTERN REVIEW, 20 (1956), 87-99.

The recollections are by people who "have all had a hand in the development of the WESTERN REVIEW at some time or another since its founding in 1936": Wallace Stegner, Grant H. Redford, George Snell, Brewster Ghiselin, M.L. Nielsen, Alan Swallow, R.W. Stallman, and R.V. Cassill. Snell's account also appears as "The Early WESTERN REVIEW," in SOUTH DAKOTA REVIEW, 6 (Autumn 1968), 37-40.

"Stock Taking." ROCKY MOUNTAIN REVIEW, 6 (Fall 1941), 2.

The editors note that they receive two subscriptions from the East for every one from a local reader. New York City is second only to Salt Lake City in number of subscribers.

W[est], R[ay] B. "Editorial Aims." ROCKY MOUNTAIN REVIEW, 7 (Spring-Summer 1943), 2.

Although the REVIEW has been willing to publish authors from other regions, "A tabulation of all material published in the REVIEW during 1942 shows that more than 50 per cent was written by Rocky Mountain authors in the following proportions: 4 out of 9 short stories, 11 out of 16 poems, and 2 of 4 articles."

______. "An Editorial Recapitulation: 20 Years." WESTERN REVIEW, 20 (1956), 83-86.

West reprints excerpts from the REVIEW's editorials, many of which reveal the journal's publishing history and editorial policies. One such is the Spring 1938 announcement of a change of title. This entire "recapitulation" also appeared in the SOUTH DAKOTA REVIEW, 6 (Autumn 1968), 26-31.

LARIAT (1923-29)

Stevens, James. "The Northwest Takes to Poesy." AMERICAN MERCURY, 16 (1929), 64-70.

Stevens pokes fun at the reactionary literary views of Colonel E. Hofer's LARIAT.

THE LAUGHING HORSE (1922-39)

Johnson, Spud. "History of 'The Laughing Horse.'" SOUTH DAKOTA REVIEW, 6 (Autumn 1968), 12-21.

Johnson founded the LAUGHING HORSE at the University of California at Berkeley with Roy Chanslor and James T. Van Rensselaer in 1922. He relates the journal's history through its twenty-one issues, including its frequent shifts in location. Johnson was responsible for developing the LAUGHING HORSE's focus on Southwestern culture.

THE NEW MEXICO QUARTERLY REVIEW (1931-49), later THE NEW MEXICO QUARTERLY (1950-69)

"Thirtieth Anniversary." NEW MEXICO QUARTERLY, 30 (1960), 109-10.

The statement of purpose from the first issue is reprinted, and the contents of that issue are discussed. The editorial history of the QUARTERLY is then briefly related.

TWENTIETH ANNIVERSARY INDEX TO THE NEW MEXICO QUARTERLY. Albuquerque: New Mexico Quarterly, 1950.

A preface briefly relates the journal's editorial and publishing history, including its merger with the NEW MEXICO BUSINESS REVIEW in 1941, and its balance of a regionalist outlook with a broader cultural interest.

THE OVERLAND MONTHLY (1868-75, 1883-1935)

Chu, Limin. "The Images of China and the Chinese in the OVERLAND MONTHLY, 1868-1875, 1883-1935." Dissertation, Duke University, 1966.

This study summarizes the relevant items and evaluates the resulting image of China and the Chinese.

Smith, Goldie Capers. "THE OVERLAND MONTHLY: Landmark in American Literature." NEW MEXICO QUARTERLY, 33 (1963), 333-40.

The final pages of this article cover the changes in policy and editorial control during the last ten years of the journal's existence. By 1930 "the journal had lost its larger regional tone, and with it, its real value."

SPACE (1934-35)

Botkin, B.A. "SPACE--after Thirty Years." CARLETON MISCELLANY, 6 (Winter 1965), 26-31.

SPACE's founder and editor discusses its history and speculates on the reasons for its demise. He feels that "SPACE had become too much the expression of one personality--my own," and that "in my eagerness to avoid the pathetic fallacy of 'the infatuation of the regionalists for the land and folk,' I had lost touch with my sources, lost the earth-contact and human interest that gave FOLK-SAY its broad appeal."

THE TEXAS REVIEW (1915-24), later THE SOUTHWEST REVIEW (1924-current)

Dobie, J. Frank. "As the Moving Finger Writ." SOUTHWEST REVIEW, 40 (1955), 289-98.

Dobie, a frequent contributor, focuses on the editorial activities of John McGinnis and Henry Nash Smith in the years after Jay Hubbell relinquished the editorship and went to Duke University. Dobie also discusses the journal's attempted balance of regional and national or international interests.

"The Editors' Notebook in Retrospect." SOUTHWEST REVIEW, 40 (1955), iv, vi-vii, 373-76.

Two previous editorials are reprinted here: Stark Young's "On Reeking of the Soil" (1915) and an excerpt from Donald Day's "Editorial" (1944). Also included are parts of Robert Adger Law's "THE TEXAS REVIEW, 1915-1924" (1924) and Jay B. Hubbell's "The New Southwest" (1924).

Hubbell, Jay B. "SOUTHWEST REVIEW, 1924-1927." SOUTHWEST REVIEW, 50 (1965), 1-18.

Hubbell discusses the editorial policies and early financial problems of the REVIEW. He became its editor in 1924 when it changed its name and moved from the University of Texas to Southern Methodist University. This essay was reprinted in Hubbell's SOUTH AND SOUTHWEST: LITERARY ESSAYS AND REMINISCENCES (Durham, N.C.: Duke University Press, 1965), pp. 3-21.

Law, Robert Adger. "THE TEXAS REVIEW, 1915-1924." SOUTHWEST REVIEW, 10 (October 1924), 83-90.

The first editor of the REVIEW relates the founding and history of the periodical.

Smith, Henry Nash. "McGinnis and the SOUTHWEST REVIEW." SOUTHWEST REVIEW, 40 (1955), 299-310.

> Smith, who worked on the REVIEW through the early 1930's, discusses the policies and problems faced by John H. McGinnis, editor from 1927 to 1941. McGinnis guided the publication with a regionalist philosophy, but at the same time printed articles on international topics.

Tinkle, Lon. "Milestone for a Magazine." SOUTHWEST REVIEW, 40 (1955), 281-88.

> Throughout its history the journal has been regional, but not provincial: "Never formulated into a program or a manifesto or a credo, this perception of a culture unique to the Southwest but kin to the parent-spirit of true culture everywhere prevailed for two decades at least in the REVIEW's policy."

Trippet, Mary Maud. "A History of the SOUTHWEST REVIEW: Toward an Understanding of Regionalism." Dissertation, University of Illinois, 1966.

# Chapter 6

# POLITICALLY RADICAL LITERARY PERIODICALS

## GENERAL STUDIES

Aaron, Daniel. WRITERS ON THE LEFT: EPISODES IN AMERICAN LITERARY COMMUNISM. New York: Harcourt, Brace & World, 1961.

This history of twentieth-century radicalism includes thorough discussions of the MASSES, the LIBERATOR, the NEW MASSES, PARTISAN REVIEW, MASSES AND MAINSTREAM, and the writers and editors who created and fostered them. Aaron argues that the NEW MASSES ultimately failed because, unlike the MASSES, it was unable to combine or accomodate political radicalism and literary aestheticism, or bohemianism. Chapters are included on Joseph Freeman, Granville Hicks, Max Eastman, and V.F. Calverton, all closely associated with various of the radical literary journals.

Fabre, Michel. "Jack Conroy as Editor." NEW LETTERS, 39 (Winter 1972), 115-37.

Conroy edited first the REBEL POET (1931-32), and then the ANVIL (1933-35) and the NEW ANVIL (1939-40). This article covers in detail Conroy's problems with the Communist party, his rivalry with Philip Rahv, who managed to take over the REBEL POET and then absorb the ANVIL with PARTISAN REVIEW, and other of his editorial experiences.

Freeman, Joseph. AN AMERICAN TESTAMENT: A NARRATIVE OF REBELS AND ROMANTICS. New York: Farrar & Rinehart, 1936.

In chapter VI of book III, "THE NEW MASSES," Freeman describes the founding of the periodical, and in pages following he refers to events relating to its publication. Also, on pages 163-68 he discusses the MASSES trials and the impression they made upon him as a college student.

Gold, Michael. "THE MASSES Tradition." MASSES AND MAINSTREAM, 4 (August 1951), 45-55.

Gold describes his involvement with the publication of the MASSES. He includes a brief history of the journal's founding by Piet Vlag, as well as an attack on editor Max Eastman, whom he considers an egotist. Gold concludes by discussing his own founding of the monthly NEW MASSES later.

Hagglund, Ben. ". . . akin to revelation. . . ." CARLETON MISCELLANY, 6 (Winter 1965), 62-68.

Hagglund, an editor and printer of little magazines during the 1930's and after World War II, discusses his work with Jack Conroy on the ANVIL and the NEW ANVIL and comments on his own short-lived poetry magazines, the NORTHERN LIGHT (1927-28) and WESTERN POETRY (1929). From 1933 to 1934 he worked in the print shop at Llano Cooperative Colony in Louisiana, where he helped to put out "a score" of little magazines.

Hicks, Granville. "Our Magazines and Their Functions." GRANVILLE HICKS IN THE NEW MASSES. Ed. Jack Alan Robbins. Port Washington, N.Y.: Kennikat Press, 1974, pp. 263-66. First published in the NEW MASSES, 18 December 1934, pp. 22-23.

Hicks feels that leftist literary journals waste money and energy through duplication of effort.

Miller, Fred R. "THE NEW MASSES and Who Else." BLUE PENCIL, 2 (February 1935), 4-5.

The editor of BLAST accuses the NEW MASSES and PARTISAN REVIEW of attempting to squeeze out all competition.

Tell, Waldo. Untitled article. PARTISAN REVIEW, 1 (1934), 60-63.

This article examines the contents of LEFT FRONT, the ANVIL, BLAST, and DYNAMO, all left-wing literary journals.

Young, Art. ART YOUNG: HIS LIFE AND TIMES. Ed. John Nicholas Beffel. New York: Sheridan House, 1939.

Chapters XXVI through XXXI cover Young's experiences on the MASSES, including a detailed account of the first sedition trial. In chapter XXXII, "Stifling the Voices against the War," he depicts the ostracization by former friends after the trials, even though all of the accused were acquitted. The unsuccessful libel suit brought by the Associated Press against editor Max Eastman and Young in 1913 is described in chapter XXVIII, "The A.P. Robes Itself in White." The history of GOOD MORNING, which Young founded and then edited from 1919 to 1922 is covered in chapter XXXIII, "Some Optimists Launch Another Magazine." His art work for the LIBERATOR is also discussed in these pages, with a detailed account in chapter XXXVI, "Battles on the LIBERATOR Board."

Zabel, Morton D[auwen]. "Recent Magazines." POETRY, 44 (1934), 168-74.

The first half of this article discusses the changes occurring among the myriad of left-wing literary periodicals.

## STUDIES OF INDIVIDUAL PERIODICALS

### THE AMERICAN REVIEW (1933-37)

Stone, Albert E., Jr. "Seward Collins and the AMERICAN REVIEW: Experiment in Pro-Fascism, 1933-37." AMERICAN QUARTERLY, 12 (1960), 3-19.

This article relates the pro-Fascist outlook presented in the REVIEW's pages, and the ideological conflict which erupted in 1936 between editor Collins and the Agrarians, who published in the journal. "Whether a sense of ideological defeat caused Collins to give up his magazine or whether he ran into financial troubles is difficult to determine."

### THE ANVIL (1932-35), THE NEW ANVIL (1939-40)

Conroy, Jack. "Days of THE ANVIL." AMERICAN BOOK COLLECTOR, 21 (Summer 1971), 15-19.

Conroy reminisces about the personalities and activities involved in the founding of the NEW ANVIL in Chicago, the first issue of which appeared in March 1939. He says little here of the first ANVIL.

Conroy, Jack, and Curt Johnson, eds. WRITERS IN REVOLT: THE ANVIL ANTHOLOGY. New York: Lawrence Hill, 1973.

Conroy, former editor of the ANVIL, provides an introduction which traces the history of the journal to its absorption by the PARTISAN REVIEW in 1935, a move which he claims was forced upon him by the Communist party. He also discusses other radical periodicals of the 1930's, including two he edited, the REBEL POET and the NEW ANVIL, the last as a protest against the earlier disappearance of the ANVIL.

BLACK & WHITE (1939-40), later THE CLIPPER: A WESTERN REVIEW (1940-41)

Endore, Guy. "BLACK & WHITE: Los Angeles, 1939-1940. THE CLIPPER: A WESTERN REVIEW: Los Angeles, 1940-1941." THE AMERICAN RADICAL PRESS, 1880-1960. Ed. Joseph R. Conlin. Westport, Conn.: Greenwood Press, 1974. II, 554-61.

Founded by Wilbur Needham and Saul Marks, with Byron Citron as editor, the journal was anti-Fascist in outlook. Its title changed when Needham resigned. Endore, who worked on the periodical, discusses its editorial content and the continuing conflicts over policy.

THE COMING NATION (1910-13)

Kreuter, Kent, and Gretchen Kreuter. "THE COMING NATION: THE MASSES' Country Cousin." AMERICAN QUARTERLY, 19 (1967), 583-86.

Founded in Girard, Kansas, in 1910 by Julius Wayland, the COUNTRY COUSIN was the first radical literary journal in America. Editors Charles Edward Russell and A.M. Simons first used drawings and cartoons as important elements, and also at times presented their views with wit and humor, two innovations which Max Eastman has claimed for the MASSES.

THE COMRADE (1901-5)

Conlin, Joseph R. "THE COMRADE: New York, 1901-1905." THE AMERICAN RADICAL PRESS, 1880-1960. Ed. Joseph R. Conlin. Westport, Conn.: Greenwood Press, 1974. II, 527-31.

This journal is considered a forerunner of the MASSES. The major difference according to Conlin, however, besides overall quality, is that "THE COMRADE, not excepting its socialism, was part and parcel of the genteel tradition, hardly avant-garde in 1901."

THE FREEMAN (1920-24)

Brooks, Van Wyck. DAYS OF THE PHOENIX: THE NINETEEN-TWENTIES I REMEMBER. New York: E.P. Dutton, 1957.

Chapter IV, "THE FREEMAN," covers the journal's policies and contents, and includes a character study of founder and editor Albert Nock. Brooks served as literary editor. This chapter is included in Brooks's AN AUTOBIOGRAPHY (New York: E.P. Dutton, 1965), pp. 304-17.

Crunden, Robert M. THE MIND AND ART OF ALBERT JAY NOCK. Chicago: Henry Regnery, 1964.

Chapter VI, "The Jeffersonian as a Radical: The FREEMAN Years, 1920-24," examines Nock's brand of radicalism as he expressed it in the FREEMAN, including the influence of Matthew Arnold's thought upon his views of the role of literature and religion in man's life. Crunden considers Francis Neilson's comments about Nock, as expressed in Neilson's "The Story of THE FREEMAN" (cited below), to be unfair and in "execrable taste" (pp. 200-202, note 40).

Neilson, Francis. MY LIFE IN TWO WORLDS. VOLUME TWO, 1915-1952. Appleton, Wis.: C.C. Nelson, 1953.

Chapter VII, "The Beginnings of THE FREEMAN," and chapter XI, "Writers in New York," briefly cover the birth and death of the journal. In chapter XII, "Literary Talent on THE FREEMAN," Neilson reminisces about the contributors who later became well known, including Llewelyn Powys, Harold Stearns, and Arthur Symons.

_____. "The Story of THE FREEMAN." Supplement to the AMERICAN JOURNAL OF ECONOMICS AND SOCIOLOGY, 6 (1946).

In this fifty-three page supplement, Neilson relates the journal's history. He focuses critically on the character of editor Albert Nock, often disagreeing with Nock's version of his own role as expressed in MEMOIRS OF A SUPERFLUOUS MAN (see below). Neilson's wife, Helen Swift Neilson, financed the publication, and Neilson himself was one of its most frequent contributors.

Nock, Albert Jay. MEMOIRS OF A SUPERFLUOUS MAN. 1943; rpt. Chicago: Henry Regnery, 1964.

Part II of chapter IX (pp. 167-74) covers Nock's founding of the FREEMAN and the policies with which he guided it. He seemed to view the enterprise as a hobby, and his passing interest is revealed in this statement: "As soon as I saw that the success of our experiment was certain and, if I may say so, that it would be rather distinguished, my interest began to dribble away."

"The Passing of the FREEMAN." NEW REPUBLIC, 5 March 1924, pp. 33-34.

The FREEMAN, although an intelligent journal, failed to gain a sufficient readership because of its cynical view of government and politics: "It is easy, after the event, to see that the FREEMAN should have put its excellent material on literature, art, and philosophy at the top of the basket and its little sour political berries at the bottom."

Tanselle, G. Thomas. "Charles A. Beard in the 'Freeman.'" PAPERS OF THE BIBLIOGRAPHICAL SOCIETY OF AMERICA, 57 (1963), 226-29.

Tanselle lists articles and book reviews, some of them under pseudonyms, that Beard contributed to the FREEMAN between July 20, 1921, and August 23, 1922.

______. "Unsigned and Initialed Contributions to THE FREEMAN." STUDIES IN BIBLIOGRAPHY, 17 (1964), 153-75.

Turner, Susan J[ane]. A HISTORY OF THE FREEMAN: LITERARY LANDMARK OF THE EARLY TWENTIES. New York: Columbia University Press, 1963.

The journal's publishing history and editorial policies are thoroughly covered. Its literary contents, which shared space with political articles, included essays by Van Wyck Brooks under the title "A Reviewer's Notebook."

______. "A Short History of THE FREEMAN, a Magazine of the Early Twenties, With Particular Attention to the Literary Criticism." Dissertation, Columbia University, 1956.

Wreszin, Michael. "Albert Jay Nock and the Anarchist Elitist Tradition in America." AMERICAN QUARTERLY, 21 (1969), 165-89.

Included in this analysis is an examination of Nock's ideas expressed in the FREEMAN and his activities as its editor.

## GOOD MORNING (1919-21)

Aaron, Daniel. "GOOD MORNING: New York, 1919-1921." THE AMERICAN RADICAL PRESS, 1880-1960. Ed. Joseph R. Conlin. Westport, Conn.: Greenwood Press, 1974. II, 585-89.

This account draws heavily from Art Young's ART YOUNG: HIS LIFE AND TIMES (see the General Studies section of this chapter, above). Aaron emphasizes the humorous tone which distinguished the journal from other radical publications.

## THE MASSES (1911-17), later THE LIBERATOR (1918-24)

Brooks, Van Wyck. JOHN SLOAN: A PAINTER'S LIFE. New York: E.P. Dutton, 1955.

Chapter VII, "Socialism: THE MASSES," describes Sloan's growing interest in socialism, his work on the MASSES, his disillusionment with the editors' doctrinaire policies, and his dissociation with the periodical in 1916.

Brown, Bob. "Them Asses." AMERICAN MERCURY, 30 (1933), 403-11.

The personalities of the MASSES editors and contributors, and the conflicts between them, are revealed in this sketch of the journal's history.

Cantor, Milton. MAX EASTMAN. New York: Twayne, 1970.

Chapter V, "The MASSES and the Guns of War," covers Eastman's activities as editor of the MASSES from 1912 to 1918 and then the LIBERATOR from 1918 to 1921. Cantor includes a discussion of Eastman's radical social articles in the MASSES and his policy of avoiding narrow and doctrinaire criteria for the journal's contents.

Dell, Floyd. "The Story of the Trial." LIBERATOR, 1 (June 1918), 17-18.

Dell discusses the first MASSES conspiracy trial.

Eastman, Max. "Bunk about Bohemia." MODERN MONTHLY, 8 (1934), 200-208.

Eastman attempts to correct misrepresentations which have been made about his editorship of the MASSES. He was accused of "Bohemianism," or "Greenwich Villagism," an aesthetic instead of revolutionary outlook.

______. ENJOYMENT OF LIVING. New York: Harper and Brothers, 1948.

Part 6 of this autobiography, "Editor and Revolutionist," covers Eastman's work on the MASSES. He discusses "The Policy of THE MASSES" (Chapter L), his money-raising efforts for the journal, and the editorial help he received from Floyd Dell.

______. "John Reed and the Old MASSES." MODERN MONTHLY, 10 (October 1936), 19-22, 31.

Eastman argues that Granville Hicks's book JOHN REED, THE MAKING OF A REVOLUTIONARY (New York: Macmillan, 1936), written from a Stalinist viewpoint, ignores the influence on Reed's revolutionary consciousness of Eastman himself and of the MASSES, and instead exaggerates the influence of Lincoln Steffens. "Preface to Max Eastman's Article" (p. 18) includes an exchange of letters written in 1935 between Eastman and Hicks, in one of which Eastman refuses to cooperate with Hicks on his Reed book and questions Hicks's objectivity.

______. LOVE AND REVOLUTION: MY JOURNEY THROUGH AN EPOCH. New York: Random House, 1964.

"Part One: 1917-1922" includes chapters on Eastman's editorship of both the MASSES and the LIBERATOR. He discusses in detail such events as the two conspiracy trials of the MASSES editors during World War I, and later his conflict with Michael Gold and his own resignation as editor of the LIBERATOR.

______. "New Masses for Old." MODERN MONTHLY, 8 (1934), 292-300.

The former editor of the MASSES argues that "this myth of my being a Greenwich Village art-rebel who went bourgeois when it came to a class choice, and that the editors of THE NEW MASSES by contrast are carrying forward the banner of proletarian revolution . . . is a piece of fabricated ballyhoo from start to finish."

Ely-Estorick, Eric, and Oscar H. Fidell. "The MASSES Tradition in Contemporary Literature." CONTEMPO, 5 April 1933, pp. 1-3, 8.

This article reviews the history of both the MASSES and the LIBERATOR and includes mention of the SEVEN ARTS.

Finkelstein, Sidney. "John Sloan: American Painter." MASSES AND MAINSTREAM, 8 (July 1955), 17-27.

This article includes information on Sloan's association with the MASSES as its art editor from 1910 to 1916. He resigned when other editors decided to make the art work more specifically political.

Fitzgerald, Richard. "MASSES: New York, 1911-1917. LIBERATOR: New York, 1918-1924." THE AMERICAN RADICAL PRESS, 1880-1960. Ed. Joseph R. Conlin. Westport, Conn.: Greenwood Press, 1974. II, 532-38.

Fitzgerald compares the editorial viewpoints of the journals, and examines the political atmosphere in which they were published. He concludes, "Compared with the MASSES, the LIBERATOR reflected the process of transition between the latitudinarian, ideologically vague, and Village-oriented American socialism of the pre-Russian Revolution years and the hard-line communism of the depression."

Hillquit, Morris. LOOSE LEAVES FROM A BUSY LIFE. New York: Macmillan, 1934.

Chapter VI of book II, "'The Masses' Trial," covers Hillquit's experiences as the defense lawyer for MASSES editors and writers in the first trial, which began in April 1918. He includes information on jury selection, courtroom procedure, and the oppressive atmosphere of the proceedings.

McKay, Claude. A LONG WAY FROM HOME. New York: Harcourt, Brace & World, 1970.

McKay's experiences while an editor of the LIBERATOR are covered in chapters IX through XII of part 3 (pp. 95-146). After Max Eastman resigned as editor, McKay shared the duties with Michael Gold, but they disagreed and McKay left the periodical.

Maik, Thomas Alan. "A History of THE MASSES Magazine." Dissertation, Bowling Green State University, 1968.

Maik attributes the high quality achieved by the periodical to editor Max Eastman. The final chapter discusses the first MASSES trial.

North, Joseph. ROBERT MINOR: ARTIST AND CRUSADER. New York: International Publishers, 1956.

"The LIBERATOR" (pp. 125-38) covers Minor's work as cartoonist and writer for that periodical. Minor also published before that in the MASSES.

O'Neill, William L., ed. ECHOES OF REVOLT: THE MASSES, 1911-1917. Chicago: Quadrangle Books, 1966.

In his general introduction (pp. 17-24) and introductions to individual sections, O'Neill covers the contents and editorial outlook of the MASSES. "To THE MASSES--With Love and Envy" by Irving Howe and "The Policy of THE MASSES, an Editor's Reflections," an afterword by Max Eastman, also discuss editorial policies. Included in the anthology are editorial statements relating to the suppression of the MASSES by the U.S. Post Office in August 1917. The wide variety of anthologized material, accompanied by reproductions of the periodical's art work, creates an accurate reflection of the quality and spirit of the MASSES.

Young, Art. ON MY WAY: BEING THE BOOK OF ART YOUNG IN TEXT AND PICTURE. New York: Horace Liveright, 1928.

On pages 274-99 Young relates the history of the MASSES, including an account of the conspiracy trials and his art work for the journal.

## THE MODERN QUARTERLY (1923-32, 1938-40), entitled THE MODERN MONTHLY (1933-38)

Genizi, Haim. "Edmund Wilson and THE MODERN MONTHLY, 1934-5: A Phase in Wilson's Radicalism." JOURNAL OF AMERICAN STUDIES, 7 (1973), 301-19.

Wilson served on the editorial board of the MODERN MONTHLY for one year, became dissatisfied with V.F. Calverton's editorial carelessness, and resigned. Wilson was initially drawn to the periodical because he shared Calverton's view that America needed a Marxist philosophy peculiar to its own cultural tradition and economic situation.

_____. "V.F. Calverton, a Radical Magazinist for Black Intellectuals, 1920-1940." JOURNAL OF NEGRO HISTORY, 57 (1972), 241-53.

Calverton befriended black intellectuals, opened the pages of his journal to their work, and wrote about the contributions of black artists and writers to the American cultural tradition.

Hook, Sidney. "THE MODERN QUARTERLY: Baltimore and New York, 1923-1932, 1938-1940. THE MODERN MONTHLY: New York, 1933-1938." THE AMERICAN RADICAL PRESS, 1880-1960. Ed. Joseph R. Conlin. Westport, Conn.: Greenwood Press, 1974. II, 596-605.

This study focuses on editor V.F. Calverton, an independent thinker who in the 1930's was constantly attacked by the Communist party in its own publications.

Ramsey, David, and Alan Calmer. "The Marxism of V.F. Calverton." NEW MASSES, 8 (January 1933), 9-27.

Calverton's political philosophy and editorial policies are attacked.

Singer, Herman. "The MODERN QUARTERLY, 1923-1940." MODERN QUARTERLY, 11 (Fall 1940), 13-19.

In this last issue of the QUARTERLY, the "V.F. Calverton Memorial Issue," Singer reviews the editorial history of the journal. Singer points out, "The question of literary values and their relationship to Marxism was one which received a regular thrashing out in the pages of the QUARTERLY through the years." He examines the views on this question expressed in the periodical.

THE NEW MASSES (1926-48)

Elistratova, A. "NEW MASSES." INTERNATIONAL LITERATURE, 1 (1932), 107-14.

Writing for the International Union of Revolutionary Writers, Elistratova accuses the NEW MASSES of failing "to fulfill its responsible role as the theoretician and guide of the proletarian and revolutionary literature in the USA."

Fitzgerald, Richard. "NEW MASSES: New York, 1926-1948." THE AMERICAN RADICAL PRESS, 1880-1960. Ed. Joseph R. Conlin. Westport, Conn.: Greenwood Press, 1974. II, 539-45.

Because of its restrictive ideological outlook, the NEW MASSES was less successful than the earlier MASSES in publishing exciting and high-quality art and literature.

Hicks, Granville. GRANVILLE HICKS IN THE NEW MASSES. Ed. Jack Alan Robbins. Port Washington, N.Y.: Kennikat Press, 1974.

The editor's introduction and "Statement by Granville Hicks in 1973" (pp. xi-xviii) present information on the history of the NEW MASSES. Hicks was literary editor from 1933 to 1939.

______. PART OF THE TRUTH. New York: Harcourt, Brace & World, 1965.

Pages 118-85 of this autobiography cover the period during which Hicks served as literary and then contributing editor of the NEW MASSES. His break with the Communist party, caused by his reaction against Soviet foreign policy, was accompanied by his break with the journal.

North, Joseph. "The MASSES Tradition." MASSES AND MAINSTREAM, 4 (September 1951), 34-41.

North, editor of the weekly NEW MASSES from 1934 to 1948, describes the struggle to keep the periodical alive in the face of economic problems and hostility from the established press. He also discusses the contributors, many of them unknown in literary circles.

______. NO MEN ARE STRANGERS. New York: International Publishers, 1958.

In chapter VIII, "I Help Found a Magazine," North discusses the change of the NEW MASSES from a monthly to a weekly, his own role in raising the necessary capital from a wealthy patron, and the editorial decision to emphasize political instead of literary journalism. Later chapters also deal incidentally with North's work for the journal.

______, ed. NEW MASSES: AN ANTHOLOGY OF THE REBEL THIRTIES. New York: International Publishers, 1969.

In a prologue North supplies background information on the journal's history, stating, "I do not see how it is possible for a just critic of NEW MASSES to judge it adequately by reading the page cold. It seems to me he must know the time, the purpose, the circumstances." Ruth McKenney's "NEW MASSES Is Home" (pp. 308-11) emotionally describes a meeting of February 26,

1940, called to fight suppression of the journal.

Novak, Estelle Gershgoren. "'New Masses': Five Yearly Indexes of the Poetry, Fiction, Criticism, Drama and Reviews for the Years 1929 through 1933." BULLETIN OF BIBLIOGRAPHY, 28 (1971), 89-108.

Each year is indexed separately, with subject indexes on poetry, fiction, criticism, drama, and reviews.

Peck, David Russell. "The Development of an American Marxist Literary Criticism: The Monthly NEW MASSES." Dissertation, Temple University, 1968.

Peck examines the criticism which appeared in the NEW MASSES from 1926 to 1933.

Unrue, John. "Hemingway and the NEW MASSES." FITZGERALD/HEMINGWAY ANNUAL 1969. Ed. Matthew J. Bruccoli. Washington, D.C.: NCR Microcard Editions, 1969, pp. 131-40.

After urging Hemingway to take their point of view during the 1930's, leftist critics of the NEW MASSES felt betrayed by the version of the Spanish Civil War portrayed in FOR WHOM THE BELL TOLLS.

PARTISAN REVIEW (1934-current)

Arrowsmith, William. "PARTISAN REVIEW and American Writing." HUDSON REVIEW, 1 (1949), 526-36.

Arrowsmith attacks what he considers to be the narrow literary views and bad writing of the REVIEW, especially since 1943.

Cowley, Malcolm. "PARTISAN REVIEW." NEW REPUBLIC, 19 October 1938, pp. 311-12.

Cowley expresses disappointment with the PARTISAN REVIEW because instead of following a policy of political independence, as stated in December 1937, it has become the mouthpiece for a narrow Trotskyist viewpoint.

Fiedler, Leslie A. "'Partisan Review': Phoenix or Dodo?" PERSPECTIVES USA, no. 15 (Spring 1956), pp. 82-97.

The writer expresses his admiration for and exasperation with the REVIEW. "Blasted into ashes by its enemies, mourned prematurely by its friends, despaired of by its own editors--it yet somehow survives; and that is, after all, the point."

Gilbert, James B[urkhart]. "PARTISAN REVIEW: New York, 1934-- ." THE AMERICAN RADICAL PRESS, 1880-1960. Ed. Joseph R. Conlin. Westport, Conn.: Greenwood Press, 1974. II, 548-53.

This article traces the history of the journal, with emphasis on the shifts in its political outlook, up to its move to Rutgers University in 1963.

______. WRITERS AND PARTISANS: A HISTORY OF LITERARY RADICALISM IN AMERICA. New York: John Wiley and Sons, 1968.

This detailed study of the PARTISAN REVIEW includes much information on the MASSES and especially the NEW MASSES, whose editors attacked the PARTISAN REVIEW in the 1930's. Gilbert examines every stage in the REVIEW's gradual break with the Communist party, and finally with political radicalism, as well as the development of the literary views of editors Phillips and Rahv and early associates, including Dwight Macdonald and Mary McCarthy.

Phillips, William, and Philip Rahv. "In Retrospect: Ten Years of PARTISAN REVIEW." THE PARTISAN READER: TEN YEARS OF PARTISAN REVIEW, 1934-1944: AN ANTHOLOGY. Ed. William Phillips and Philip Rahv. New York: Dial Press, 1946, pp. 679-88.

The editors relate the PARTISAN REVIEW's history, focusing on their growing disenchantment with Stalinism, which led to the suspension of publication in the fall of 1936. They then explain the new policies of the revived REVIEW, its economic struggles, and its changes in personnel.

Trilling, Lionel. "The Function of the Little Magazine." THE LIBERAL IMAGINATION: ESSAYS ON LITERATURE AND SOCIETY. New York: Viking Press, 1950, pp. 93-103.

Trilling examines the gap between the general educated class and the literary class that has developed in the twentieth century, and he argues that "to organize a new union between our political ideas and our imagination--in all our cultural purview there is no work more necessary. It is to this work that PARTISAN REVIEW has devoted itself for more than a decade." This essay first appeared as the introduction to THE PARTISAN READER: TEN YEARS OF PARTISAN REVIEW, 1934-1944: AN ANTHOLOGY (see Phillips and Rahv, above).

Wald, Alan. "Revolutionary Intellectuals: PARTISAN REVIEW in the 1930's." OCCIDENT, 8 (Spring 1974), 118-33.

Wright, Elizabeth, and PARTISAN REVIEW staff. PARTISAN REVIEW INDEX: CUMULATIVE COMPILATION, 1934-1965, VOLS. 1-31. New York: AMS

Reprint Co., 1967.

This index is divided into "Articles and Other Comment," "Fiction," "Verse," "Book Reviews," "Books Reviewed," "Symposia, Discussion and Exchanges," and "PARTISAN REVIEW Statements."

# Chapter 7

# ACADEMIC QUARTERLIES OF SCHOLARSHIP AND CRITICISM

## GENERAL STUDIES

Bixler, Paul. "An Audience for Standards." AMERICAN SCHOLAR, 15 (1946), 552-53.

The chairman of the editorial board of the ANTIOCH REVIEW discusses the differences between the small quarterly and the little magazine, a consideration prompted by the omission of any mention of his own journal in Hoffman, Allen, and Ulrich, THE LITTLE MAGAZINE: A HISTORY AND A BIBLIOGRAPHY (see the General Studies section of Chapter 4).

Brandt, Joseph A., et al. "The Reader's Forum: The Misery and Necessity of the Quarterly." AMERICAN SCHOLAR, 16 (1946-47), 104-7.

Brandt, Henry W. Simon, Allen Tate, and Lionel Trilling give their views on the function of the literary quarterly in America. They are responding to articles on the same subject by John Crowe Ransom, Paul Bixler, and Delmore Schwartz which appeared in previous issues of the AMERICAN SCHOLAR (Bixler's and Schwartz's articles are listed in this section, and Ransom's is listed in the General Studies section of chapter 4).

Colvert, James B. "The Function of the Academic Critical Quarterly." MISSISSIPPI QUARTERLY, 23 (1969-70), 95-101.

The editor of the GEORGIA REVIEW defends academic quarterlies against various charges, and concludes, "The only defensible policy of the academic critical quarterly is to be wholeheartedly academic. Its purpose is to extend to its readers the best that is being thought and said in the university community, and if this purpose is unworthy, then it is because the university itself is unworthy."

Newman, William J. "The American Literary Review." TWENTIETH CENTURY, 155 (1954), 342-50.

Newman discusses the pros and cons of the established reviews which are increasingly supported by and draw their contributors from the universities.

Rice, Philip Blair. "The Intellectual Quarterly in a Non-Intellectual Society." KENYON REVIEW, 16 (1954), 420-39.

Rice discusses the cultural importance of journals such as the PARTISAN, SEWANEE, HUDSON, and KENYON reviews.

Schwartz, Delmore. "An Unpleasant and Important Fact." AMERICAN SCHOLAR, 15 (1946), 553-54.

An editor of PARTISAN REVIEW emphasizes the importance of the literary quarterly in America despite its small circulation.

Tate, Allen. "The Function of the Critical Quarterly." SOUTHERN REVIEW, 1 (1936), 551-59.

The quarterly's main function "is not to give the public what it wants, or what it thinks it wants, but what--through the medium of its most intelligent members--it ought to have." Tate also discusses the problems faced by the quarterly and its editor, the chief of which is the competition with the monthlies and weeklies for talent and readership.

## STUDIES OF INDIVIDUAL PERIODICALS

### AMERICAN LITERATURE (1929-current)

Hubbell, Jay B. "AMERICAN LITERATURE, 1928-1954." SOUTH AND SOUTHWEST: LITERARY ESSAYS AND REMINISCENCES. Durham, N.C.: Duke University Press, 1965, pp. 22-48.

Hubbell, managing editor of AMERICAN LITERATURE from 1929 until 1954, relates in detail the events leading to its founding at Duke University, and its editorial goals and policies over the years. He includes an account of a rival proposal for a similar journal which was to be published at Brown University. This proposal was rejected by the American Literature Group of the Modern Language Association in favor of the Duke proposal.

Marshall, Thomas F. AN ANALYTICAL INDEX TO AMERICAN LITERATURE, VOLUMES I-XXX: MARCH 1929-JANUARY 1959. Durham, N.C.: Duke University Press, 1963.

Marshall revises and expands his twenty-year index, published in 1954. Part 1 is an author-subject index and part 2 a book review index.

THE HUDSON REVIEW (1948-current)

Morgan, Frederick, ed. THE MODERN IMAGE: OUTSTANDING STORIES FROM THE HUDSON REVIEW. New York: W.W. Norton, 1965.

In an introduction (pp. 7-14) Robert M. Adams discusses the HUDSON REVIEW's editorial policy toward fiction: "In its first issue the magazine laid down as its guiding principles awareness of objective frames and traditional insights combined with a devotion to the fresh and original . . . offering as many openings as one could wish for the Protean quality of intelligence to manifest itself, setting its face only against the private hallucination, the unformed enthusiasm, the fervor of pseudo-primitivism."

THE KENYON REVIEW (1939-70)

Browne, Elizabeth, comp. KENYON REVIEW INDEX: 25 YEAR CUMULATIVE COMPILATION, 1939-1963. New York: AMS Reprint Co., 1964.

Clarke, Donald Lloyd. "John Crowe Ransom: Editor." Dissertation, Texas Christian University, 1972.

Clarke examines Ransom's editorship of the KENYON REVIEW and concludes that he had a great influence on the development of the New Criticism. Ransom's earlier involvement with the FUGITIVE is also studied.

Ransom, John Crowe, ed. THE KENYON CRITICS: STUDIES IN MODERN LITERATURE FROM THE KENYON REVIEW. Cleveland: World Publishing Co., 1951.

In his introduction Ransom notes the inevitable disappointment, in spite of his achievements, that any journal editor feels: "He remembers that an issue never did measure up with anything like evenness to the perfection which had been dreamed for it."

MODERN LANGUAGE NOTES (1886-1961), later M L N (1962-current)

Kuhl, E.P.; R.A. Parker; and H.H. Shapiro, comps. MODERN LANGUAGE NOTES: GENERAL INDEX OF VOLUMES I-L. Baltimore, Md.: Johns Hopkins Press, 1935; H.H. Shapiro and H.C. Lancaster, comps. MODERN LANGUAGE NOTES: GENERAL INDEX OF VOLUMES LI-LX. Baltimore, Md.: Johns Hopkins Press, 1946.

In his forewords to these indexes, H. Carrington Lancaster discusses the editorial policies of A. Marshall Elliot, founder and editor until 1916. He also lists the names and dates of subsequent editors.

Macksey, Richard, ed. VELOCITIES OF CHANGE: CRITICAL ESSAYS FROM MLN. Baltimore, Md.: Johns Hopkins University Press, 1974.

In the introduction, entitled "Velocities of Change" (pp. vii-xxvii), Macksey briefly sketches the journal's editorial history.

THE SEWANEE REVIEW (1892-current)

Knickerbocker, William S. "Trent at Sewanee." SEWANEE REVIEW, 48 (1940), 145-52.

His successor as editor of the SEWANEE REVIEW recounts William Peterfield Trent's achievements in the journal and at the university before Trent moved to New York.

______. "Up from the South." WESTERN REVIEW, 13 (1949), 169-78.

Knickerbocker, editor of the SEWANEE REVIEW from 1926 to 1942, discusses the outlook of the fugitive group and his editorial relationship with them.

McBryde, John M., Jr. "Twenty-Five Years of the SEWANEE REVIEW." SEWANEE REVIEW, 25 (1917), 511-12.

In this short tribute to his journal, the editor reveals an earlier struggle to keep the publication completely literary. He also gives statistics on where the contributions come from.

Munson, Gorham. "THE SEWANEE REVIEW: From 1892 to 1930." SEWANEE REVIEW, 40 (1932), 1-4.

Munson briefly surveys the journal's history and discusses its current editorial policies.

Turner, Alice Lucille. "The SEWANEE REVIEW." SEWANEE REVIEW, 40 (1932), 129-38, 257-75.

The journal's editorial and publishing history is covered, with the focus on the policies and writings of the various editors. This article is the first chapter of the author's dissertation (see below).

______. A STUDY OF THE CONTENT OF THE SEWANEE REVIEW, WITH HISTORICAL INTRODUCTION. Nashville, Tenn.: George Peabody College for Teachers, 1931.

This is Turner's dissertation, completed at Peabody in the same year.

THE YALE REVIEW (1892-current)

Cross, Wilbur L. CONNECTICUT YANKEE: AN AUTOBIOGRAPHY. New Haven, Conn.: Yale University Press, 1943.

Chapter XV, "The YALE REVIEW," covers Cross's experiences as editor of that journal from 1911 until 1940, including the resulting associations with writers and intellectuals in Europe as well as America.

______. "Our First Thirty Years." YALE REVIEW, 31 (1941), 1-8.

Although this reminiscence does not contain much specific factual material, Cross does mention the contributions to the YALE REVIEW which he feels have been most significant.

______. "Our Historical Antecedents." YALE REVIEW, 31 (1942), 645-48.

The editor relates the REVIEW's publishing history, including the transfer of the copyright to the Yale Publishing Association in 1911, and then a later transfer to the Yale University Press in 1926. He also briefly discusses earlier Yale serial publications.

______. "THE YALE REVIEW Comes of Age." YALE REVIEW, 21 (1931), 1-9.

In a world shaken by war, "it will be the purpose of THE YALE REVIEW to advance peaceful civilization by an attempt to increase and synthesize general knowledge, to encourage reasoned thinking, and to liberate the creative powers, which always have been and always will be the chief glory of the race."

"THE YALE REVIEW." HOUND & HORN, 1 (1927), 179-80.

After reviewing the first number of volume XVII (October 1927), this short article concludes that "the value of the YALE REVIEW . . . has been its consistent publication of the best non-experimental writing--of writing generally accepted as good."

YALE REVIEW INDEX. VOLUMES I-XIX. 1892-1911. New Haven, Conn.: Yale Publishing Association, 1911.

"THE YALE REVIEW in 1950." YALE REVIEW, 40 (1950), 3-5.

The editors discuss the importance and precarious existence of journals like the YALE REVIEW: "The general review, appealing primarily to the intelligence of readers at large, has been peculiarly vulnerable. It has been exposed to attack not only by the mass magazines, but by the specialized publications as well."

# Chapter 8

# BIBLIOGRAPHIES AND CHECKLISTS

## GENERAL

Ditzion, Sidney. "The History of Periodical Literature in the United States: A Bibliography." BULLETIN OF BIBLIOGRAPHY, 15 (1935), 110, 124-33.

The focus here is on literary periodicals. "The bases of selection have been authority, scholarship, length, and importance as 'new' material."

Eichelberger, Clayton L., comp. A GUIDE TO CRITICAL REVIEWS OF UNITED STATES FICTION, 1870-1910. 2 vols. Metuchen, N.J.: Scarecrow Press, 1971.

"The periodicals covered here were selected with the long-range objective, not fully realized in this single volume, of representing major American and English review outlets and lesser publications reflecting regional interests." The following periodicals are among those indexed: ATLANTIC, the BOOKMAN, HARPER'S, the NORTH AMERICAN REVIEW, the OVERLAND MONTHLY, POET LORE, the SEWANEE REVIEW, the SOUTH ATLANTIC QUARTERLY.

Gerstenberger, Donna, and George Henrick, comps. THIRD DIRECTORY OF PERIODICALS PUBLISHING ARTICLES ON ENGLISH AND AMERICAN LITERATURE AND LANGUAGE. Chicago: Swallow Press, 1970.

This directory of 547 periodicals provides information useful to prospective contributors. Included is information on desired length of manuscripts, payment rates and "major fields of interest." The first DIRECTORY appeared in 1960, with a "1962 Supplement" published in TWENTIETH CENTURY LITERATURE, 9 (1963), 89-92. The SECOND DIRECTORY appeared in 1965.

Keller, Dean H. INDEX TO PLAYS IN PERIODICALS. Metuchen, N.J.: Scarecrow Press, 1971; SUPPLEMENT, 1973.

Among the 103 periodicals indexed here, Keller includes a variety of literary journals, among them the ATLANTIC, BROOM, FURIOSO, the TEXAS REVIEW, and the YALE REVIEW. All are indexed from their first volumes through their last or 1969 volumes. The SUPPLEMENT extends the index through 1971.

O'Brien, Edward J., ed. THE BEST SHORT STORIES OF . . . AND THE YEARBOOK OF THE AMERICAN SHORT STORY. Boston: Small, Maynard, 1915-25; New York: Dodd, Mead, 1926-32; Boston: Houghton Mifflin, 1933-41.

Among the chapters in the yearbook section of his anthologies, O'Brien includes an index of short stories published in various periodicals, and "Magazine Averages," in which he rates periodicals according to the quality of their fiction. The volumes published under other editors after 1941 do not continue these chapters.

Stephens, Ethel, comp. AMERICAN POPULAR MAGAZINES: A BIBLIOGRAPHY. Boston: Boston Book Co., 1916.

Items under such headings as "Scope and Influence" could be useful in a study of literary periodicals.

Zabel, Morton Dauwen. "Appendix III: American Magazines Publishing Criticism." LITERARY OPINION IN AMERICA: ESSAYS ILLUSTRATING THE STATUS, METHODS, AND PROBLEMS OF CRITICISM IN THE UNITED STATES IN THE TWENTIETH CENTURY. Ed. Morton Dauwen Zabel. 3rd ed. New York: Harper & Row, 1962. II, 812-21.

"This check-list includes the most important magazines that have published the work of American critics since 1900. A number of standard magazines are included, but a point has been made of including the best of the independent journals and 'little magazines' that have encouraged literary experiment and critical activity. The dates and personnel of these have been described as closely as their irregular careers permit."

## LITTLE MAGAZINES OF POETRY, FICTION, AND ART

Goode, Stephen H., comp. INDEX TO LITTLE MAGAZINES 1943-1947. Denver: Alan Swallow, 1965; INDEX TO LITTLE MAGAZINES, 1940-1942. New York: Johnson Reprint, 1967; INDEX TO AMERICAN LITTLE MAGAZINES 1920-1939. Troy, N.Y.: Whitston, 1969; INDEX TO AMERICAN LITTLE MAGAZINES, 1900-1919: TO WHICH IS ADDED A SELECTED LIST OF BRITISH AND CONTINENTAL TITLES FOR THE YEARS 1900-1950, TOGETHER WITH ADDENDA AND CORRIGENDA TO PREVIOUS INDEXES. 3 vols. Troy, N.Y.: Whitston, 1974.

These are author-subject indexes of selected periodicals. Editorials, graphic art, and reviews are not indexed.

Moss, David. "A Bibliography of the Little Magazines Published in America since 1900." CONTACT, 1 (February 1932), 91-109; (May 1932), 111-24; (October 1932), 134-39.

This bibliography includes editors, dates of publication, and location.

Sader, Marion, ed. COMPREHENSIVE INDEX TO ENGLISH-LANGUAGE LITTLE MAGAZINES 1890-1970. Series 1. 8 vols. Millwood, N.Y.: Kraus-Thomson, 1976.

This index of one hundred foreign and American little magazines is organized alphabetically by contributor.

Swallow, Alan, et al., comps. INDEX TO LITTLE MAGAZINES. Denver: Alan Swallow, 1949-70.

This yearly index includes the contents of selected periodicals for the years 1948 to 1967.

Ulrich, Carolyn F., and Eugenia Patterson. "Little Magazines." BULLETIN OF THE NEW YORK PUBLIC LIBRARY, 51 (1947), 3-25. Published as a pamphlet. New York: New York Public Library, 1947.

"This list includes those periodicals which have been non-commercial though not amateur, inclined to be rebellious and more open to experimental and 'advanced' contributions than their more staid, and more stable, contemporaries. Borderline cases have been grouped in a supplement." This bibliography, which includes dates and locations, is based on that from Hoffman, Allen, and Ulrich, THE LITTLE MAGAZINE: A HISTORY AND A BIBLIOGRAPHY (see the General Studies section of Chapter 4).

See also GALLEY; THE LITTLE MAGAZINE QUARTERLY, cited in the General Studies section of Chapter 4.

## REGIONAL LITERARY PERIODICALS

Atchison, Ray M. "Southern Literary Periodicals, 1732-1967." A BIBLIOGRAPHICAL GUIDE TO THE STUDY OF SOUTHERN LITERATURE. Ed. Louis D. Rubin, Jr. Baton Rouge: Louisiana State University Press, 1969, pp. 82-89.

Atchison lists secondary sources relating to the periodicals.

Griffin, Max L. "A Bibliography of New Orleans Magazines." LOUISIANA HISTORICAL QUARTERLY, 18 (1935), 493-556.

This is an annotated bibliography of magazines that are "of some literary significance and interest." It includes a "Chronological Check-List" from 1834 to 1930 and an "Index of Editors and Principal Contributors."

## POLITICALLY RADICAL LITERARY PERIODICALS

Goldwater, Walter. RADICAL PERIODICALS IN AMERICA, 1890-1950: WITH A GENEALOGICAL CHART AND A CONCISE LEXICON OF THE PARTIES AND GROUPS WHICH ISSUED THEM. New Haven, Conn.: Yale University Library, 1966.

"Literary magazines, unless the political aspect is dominant," are excluded from this annotated bibliography. However, Goldwater does include journals such as the MASSES and the NEW MASSES. The annotations give information on editors, policies, contributors, and political affiliations. A less complete list appeared under the same title in the YALE UNIVERSITY LIBRARY GAZETTE, 37 (1963), 133-77.

# Chapter 9

## BACKGROUND STUDIES

Blankenship, Russell. AMERICAN LITERATURE AS AN EXPRESSION OF THE NATIONAL MIND. Rev. ed. New York: Henry Holt, 1949.

Blankenship's literary history focuses on "the historical and social significance of our national letters," a conception that "entails a reappraisal of our whole literature," since "whether our literature is 'great' or not is of comparatively slight importance."

Bosworth, Allan R. "The Golden Age of Pulps." ATLANTIC, 208 (July 1961), 57-60.

A former writer of pulp fiction recounts his experiences with the magazines which thrived during the 1930's and then died out during World War II.

Brooks, Van Wyck. THE CONFIDENT YEARS: 1885-1915. New York: E.P. Dutton, 1952.

In the second half of this literary and cultural history, Brooks includes the chapters "Chicago: 1910," "Mencken in Baltimore," and "Greenwich Village," all of which serve as useful background to the study of literary journalism.

Calverton, V.F. THE LIBERATION OF AMERICAN LITERATURE. New York: Charles Scribner's Sons, 1932.

Calverton feels that not until the twentieth century did American literature free itself from a "colonial complex" and petty bourgeois Puritan value system. In part 7 of chapter VI, "From Sectionalism to Nationalism," he discusses the MASSES, the LIBERATOR, the NEW MASSES, and their contribution to the development of a proletarian literature. He does criticize the MASSES for not being revolutionary enough, and the NEW MASSES for promoting literature of poor quality merely because it is revolutionary.

Churchill, Allen. THE LITERARY DECADE. Englewood Cliffs, N.J.: Prentice-Hall, 1971.

This literary history of the 1920's includes a discussion of H.L. Mencken, George Jean Nathan, and the AMERICAN MERCURY (pp. 152-73).

Commager, Henry Steele. THE AMERICAN MIND: AN INTERPRETATION OF AMERICAN THOUGHT AND CHARACTER SINCE THE 1880'S. New Haven, Conn.: Yale University Press, 1950.

Commager examines the development of twentieth-century literature in the course of his study.

"The Conduct of American Magazines." ATLANTIC, 86 (1900), 425-27.

An "outsider, who is not an editor, and but barely an author," criticizes editors for the restrictions of length and content which they place upon contributions. He then calls for "a subsidized magazine which is prepared to pay no dividends and to lose large sums monthly for the sake of printing any really good work, no matter whether it is long or short, conventional or not."

"The Confessions of a Magazine Writer." BOOKMAN, 26 (1907), 316-20.

An anonymous writer of articles, fiction, and verse tells how he broke into the magazine field, primarily by accomodating his work to the tastes and policies of editors.

Drewry, John E. CONCERNING THE FOURTH ESTATE. Athens: University of Georgia Press, 1942.

In chapter VIII, "American Magazines Today: A Survey of Periodical Journalism," Drewry touches upon matters such as the circulation figures of literary periodicals and their popularity compared to that of mass-circulation magazines.

Duffield, Marcus. "The Pulps: Day Dreams for the Masses." VANITY FAIR, 40 (June 1933), 26-27, 51, 60.

This illustrated article examines the editorial policies of the all-fiction pulp magazines, and conjectures on their readership.

Goodstone, Tony, ed. THE PULPS: FIFTY YEARS OF AMERICAN POP CULTURE. New York: Chelsea House, 1970.

Goodstone's introduction to this illustrated anthology discusses the economic and editorial history of these magazines.

Goulart, Ron. CHEAP THRILLS: AN INFORMAL HISTORY OF THE PULP

MAGAZINES. New Rochelle, N.Y.: Arlington House, 1972.

This book offers "a general outline of the whole history of the pulp magazines and a more detailed account of one specific period in that history. The detailed period is . . . roughly from 1920 to 1940."

Hersey, Harold Brainerd. PULPWOOD EDITOR. New York: Frederick A. Stokes, 1937.

An editor of many pulpwood fiction magazines describes all aspects of the business, from economics to the personalities of various pulp authors.

Hicks, Granville. THE GREAT TRADITION: AN INTERPRETATION OF AMERICAN LITERATURE SINCE THE CIVIL WAR. Rev. ed. New York: Macmillan, 1935.

This literary history focuses on the development of proletarian literature.

Hoffman, Frederick J. THE TWENTIES: AMERICAN WRITING IN THE POSTWAR DECADE. Rev. ed. New York: Free Press, 1965.

Chapter I of part 3, "VANITY FAIR: Handbook for the Sophisticate," views the periodical as an amalgam of the literary and intellectual ideas which characterized the 1920's.

Horton, Rod W., and Herbert W. Edwards. BACKGROUNDS OF AMERICAN LITERARY THOUGHT. 2nd ed. New York: Appleton-Century-Crofts, 1967.

"The purpose of this book is to provide in compact and relatively simplified form certain historical and intellectual materials necessary to a fuller understanding of the leading American authors."

Jones, Archer. "The Pulps--A Mirror to Yearning." NORTH AMERICAN REVIEW, 246 (1938), 35-47.

Archer surveys the proliferation of pulp magazines since World War I, and then analyzes generally the fiction found in them.

Jones, Howard Mumford, and Richard M. Ludwig. GUIDE TO AMERICAN LITERATURE AND ITS BACKGROUNDS SINCE 1890. 4th ed., rev. Cambridge, Mass.: Harvard University Press, 1972.

Chapter VI, "Critical List of Magazines," includes many literary journals, the histories and contents of which are described in one or two sentences.

Kazin, Alfred. ON NATIVE GROUNDS: AN INTERPRETATION OF MODERN

AMERICAN PROSE LITERATURE. New York: Reynal & Hitchcock, 1942.

This history covers the writers and the literary trends from the 1890's through the 1930's. Kazin strives to avoid the narrowness of sociological criticism on the one hand and aesthetic New Criticism on the other.

Knight, Grant C. AMERICAN LITERATURE AND CULTURE. New York: Ray Long & Richard R. Smith, 1932.

"Part Three--The Literature of Realism" covers writers and poets of the twentieth century and includes a short discussion of "Newspapers and Magazines" (pp. 491-92).

______. THE STRENUOUS AGE IN AMERICAN LITERATURE. Chapel Hill: University of North Carolina Press, 1954.

Knight examines the literary and cultural developments of the first decade of the twentieth century.

Kosinski, Jerzy. "Packaged Passion." AMERICAN SCHOLAR, 42 (1973), 193-204.

Kosinski examines confession magazines and concludes that "they reveal a significant popular need for yet another soporific: a literature that can defuse the imagination, dismiss emotion, and ultimately leave the reader disarmed, unable to face his very self or to cope with the unknown--his own existence."

Laski, Harold J. THE AMERICAN DEMOCRACY: A COMMENTARY AND AN INTERPRETATION. New York: Viking Press, 1948.

On pages 664-68 of chapter XIII, "Press, Cinema, and Radio in America," Laski briefly discusses the importance of literary magazines to American society, with special emphasis on the ATLANTIC, HARPER'S, and the AMERICAN MERCURY.

Lohr, Lenox R. MAGAZINE PUBLISHING. Baltimore, Md.: Williams & Wilkins, 1932.

This study is intended to be a handbook for newcomers to magazine publishing. Chapters are included on editorial room operations, printing, types of paper and ink, advertising sales and relations, illustration, and circulation.

MacMullen, Margaret. "Pulps and Confessions." HARPER'S, 175 (1937), 94-102.

This article surveys the fiction of the romance and adventure pulp magazines, and conjectures on those who read them. "It is not a happy picture; for sharply as these magazines differ in appeal and emphasis, they are all alike in one thing, a denial of reality."

Morris, Lloyd. POSTSCRIPT TO YESTERDAY. AMERICA: THE LAST FIFTY YEARS. New York: Random House, 1947.

Morris attempts "to sketch the principal social changes that took place in American life between 1896 and 1946, and consider what their effect has been on our minds and hearts." Chapter IX, "'Raising the Tone of Democracy,'" discusses periodicals, among them McCLURE'S.

Pattee, Fred Lewis. THE NEW AMERICAN LITERATURE, 1890-1930. New York: Century, 1930.

This literary history includes a chapter, "The New Journalism" (pp. 49-63), which recounts the founding of McCLURE'S and MUNSEY'S, and George Horace Lorimer's editorship of the SATURDAY EVENING POST. Chapter XXVIII, "Newspaper By-Products," covers the development of the literary, or semiliterary, newspaper column.

Porterfield, Ruth L. "Memoirs of a Wood Pulp Editor." AMERICAN MERCURY, 33 (1934), 180-84.

This is a humorous account of the activities involved in publishing a pulp magazine.

Quinn, Arthur Hobson, ed. THE LITERATURE OF THE AMERICAN PEOPLE: AN HISTORICAL AND CRITICAL SURVEY. New York: Appleton-Century-Crofts, 1951.

Part 4, "The Twentieth Century," includes the chapters "The Conscience of Liberalism," "The Resurgent South," "Proletarian Leanings," and "New Movements in Poetry," all of which serve as background to the study of modern literary journals.

Regier, C.C. THE ERA OF THE MUCKRAKERS. Gloucester, Mass.: Peter Smith, 1957.

Chapter II, "The Rise of the Popular Magazine," covers the founding of MUNSEY'S, McCLURE'S, COSMOPOLITAN, and the ARENA, among others. Much of the rest of Regier's study is based on the contents of these and other periodicals.

Smith, Bernard. FORCES IN AMERICAN CRITICISM: A STUDY IN THE HISTORY OF AMERICAN LITERARY THOUGHT. New York: Harcourt, Brace, 1939.

Included in this study are the sections "Socialism: Floyd Dell" (pp. 285-301) and "The Urban Tory: Mencken" (pp. 302-13), the first presenting information on the MASSES and the second on the AMERICAN MERCURY. "Liberalism and Van Wyck Brooks" (pp. 313-28) includes a discussion of the NATION's literary views under Carl Van Doren, and "The Quest for Beauty" (pp. 347-59) covers little magazines of the 1920's, including POETRY, the LITTLE REVIEW, BROOM, TRANSITION, and the DIAL.

Spiller, Robert E., et al., eds. LITERARY HISTORY OF THE UNITED STATES. 3rd ed., rev. New York: Macmillan, 1963.

This is the most basic and thorough of American literary histories.

______. LITERARY HISTORY OF THE UNITED STATES: BIBLIOGRAPHY. 4th ed., rev. 2 vols. New York: Macmillan, 1974.

"The selective bibliographies herein assembled are an integral part of the text of the History, and their organization has been determined by its form and content. At the same time, their scope is not limited by that fact. They are intended as a guide to the present state of resources and scholarship in American literary culture."

Stevenson, Elizabeth. BABBITTS AND BOHEMIANS: THE AMERICAN 1920'S. New York: Macmillan, 1967.

In chapter 1, "Identity of a Decade," the author states, "This chronicle of the American twenties takes off from the assumption that the past means something to the present, the meaning not hortatory but esthetic; that the particular past of the twenties had some coherence in its unrolling; that the elements of the time were out of gear in some large way, business on top, politics and culture allowed on sufferance. . . ." Literary journals are at times included in this portrait.

Tebbel, John. THE AMERICAN MAGAZINE: A COMPACT HISTORY. New York: Hawthorn, 1969.

This one-volume history covers the field from its beginnings through the twentieth century, and includes information on many literary journals. It is intended for the general reader and contains no footnotes or extensive bibliography.

Wish, Harvey. SOCIETY AND THOUGHT IN MODERN AMERICA. 2nd ed. 2 vols. New York: David McKay, 1962.

This study offers a thorough background on the social and intellectual milieu in which literary journals were published.

Wolseley, Roland E. THE MAGAZINE WORLD: AN INTRODUCTION TO MAGAZINE JOURNALISM. New York: Prentice-Hall, 1951.

This book provides general information on magazine economics, readership, and editorial activities. In chapter V, "Class Magazines," Wolseley includes brief sections entitled "The Quality Group" (the ATLANTIC, CENTURY, HARPER'S, and SCRIBNER'S), "The Little Magazines," and "THE NEW YORKER."

# Appendix
# LITERARY MATERIAL IN NONLITERARY PERIODICALS

## GENERAL STUDIES

Berelson, Bernard, and Patricia J. Salter. "Majority and Minority Americans: An Analysis of Magazine Fiction." PUBLIC OPINION QUARTERLY, 10 (1946), 168-90.

> Fiction in the following periodicals is analyzed: The SATURDAY EVENING POST, COLLIER'S, AMERICAN, COSMOPOLITAN, WOMAN'S HOME COMPANION, LADIES' HOME JOURNAL, TRUE STORY, and TRUE CONFESSIONS. The conclusion is that "even here, in ephemeral fiction fashioned of sweetness and light and designed purely for entertainment and divertissement, a subtle discrimination against minorities and foreigners has found its way."

Bucco, Martin. "The Serialized Novels of Sinclair Lewis." WESTERN AMERICAN LITERATURE, 4 (1969), 29-37.

> Lewis contributed fiction to periodicals such as REDBOOK, WOMAN'S HOME COMPANION, and the SATURDAY EVENING POST, willingly allowing editorial deletions of political, sexual, and religious references which might be offensive to their readers.

Deats, Ruth Z. "Poetry for the Populace: Trends in Poetic Thought in American Popular Magazines." SEWANEE REVIEW, 50 (1942), 374-88.

> The writer examines 473 poems from AMERICAN MAGAZINE, GOOD HOUSEKEEPING, HOLLAND'S, LADIES' HOME JOURNAL, McCALL'S, REDBOOK, the SATURDAY EVENING POST, and WOMAN'S HOME COMPANION. She concludes: "There is enough poetry which can be genuinely labelled 'good'; there is enough healthy experimentation going forward to prevent poetry decaying from static taste; there is enough interest on the part of two members of the poetry corporation--the magazine editor and the reader--to keep the third one--the poet--encouraged in his work."

Geist, Joseph E. "The Critical Reception of Graham Greene in Selected American Catholic Periodicals, 1930-1970." Dissertation, University of Kansas, 1972.

Although there is no unanimity of attitude toward Greene's work, Catholic critics have shown a growing understanding of his orthodox themes.

Johns-Heine, Patricke, and Hans H. Gerth. "Values in Mass Periodical Fiction, 1921-1940." PUBLIC OPINION QUARTERLY, 13 (1949), 105-13.

After evaluating fictional heroes in the ATLANTIC, COUNTRY GENTLEMAN, LADIES' HOME JOURNAL, the SATURDAY EVENING POST, and TRUE STORY, the authors conclude that "post-World War I expansiveness and optimism, long identified as archetypal of national characteristics, gave way in the 'thirties to more traditionalist values, presumably under the impact of economic depression on the one hand, and political pessimism on the other."

Zeitlin, Jacob, and Homer Woodbridge. LIFE AND LETTERS OF STUART P. SHERMAN. 2 vols. 1929; rpt. Freeport, N.Y.: Books for Libraries Press, 1971.

Chapter X in volume 1, "The 'Evening Post' and the 'Nation,'" covers Sherman's work as a literary critic and book reviewer in the early years of this century. Chapter XXX in volume 2, "Literary Editor," discusses his activities as editor in the mid-1920's of "Books," the literary supplement to the New York HERALD TRIBUNE.

## STUDIES OF INDIVIDUAL PERIODICALS

### AMERICAN FIELD SERVICE MAGAZINE (1917-19, First Series)

Graham, Walter. "Poets of the American Ambulance." SOUTH ATLANTIC QUARTERLY, 19 (1920), 18-23.

Graham reviews the poetry of American ambulance drivers published in the FIELD SERVICE BULLETIN during World War I.

### COLLIER'S (1888-1957)

COLLIER'S BEST: A SELECTION OF SHORT STORIES FROM THE MAGAZINE. New York: Harper and Brothers, 1951.

In an introduction (pp. vii-xv), Knox Burger, fiction editor of COLLIER'S, discusses the policies concerning fiction, and the editorial procedures followed for evaluation of contributions.

Davenport, Walter. "If You're Thinking of Writing for Us." THE WRITER'S HANDBOOK. Ed. A.S. Burack. Boston: The Writer, 1952, pp. 63-68.

The editor of COLLIER'S discusses the kind of fiction preferred for publication in his periodical. Good taste and entertainment value are the two main considerations.

Garraty, John A. "Henry Cabot Lodge and COLLIER'S: A Study in American Taste." WESTERN HUMANITIES REVIEW, 7 (1953), 305-12.

Garraty discusses Lodge's literary taste as revealed in his role as a judge for a COLLIER'S short story contest in 1905. Lodge rejected the choices of the other two judges, Walter Hines Page and William Allen White, who picked weak and sentimental stories.

Oberfirst, Robert. "Analysis of a COLLIER'S Short-Short Story." WRITER, 53 (1940), 172-74, 192.

Oberfirst analyzes "The Bride Looked Sad" by Quentin Reynolds, a story based on character development instead of a surprise twist in the plot. "Many smooth-paper magazines . . . are slowly doing away with the O. Henry type of short-short story with the mechanical, gag-type of ending, and are publishing the character short-short."

Sullivan, Mark. THE EDUCATION OF AN AMERICAN. New York: Doubleday, Doran, 1938.

Chapters XXIII through XXXI (pp. 204-317) cover the early history of COLLIER'S, which Sullivan wrote for, and then edited from 1914 to 1917. He says of his editorial tenure, "I gave more and more of my time to contacts with writers of fiction, less to politics. For some years authors and their writings were my major interest."

THE CRISIS (1910-34)

Yellin, Jean Fagan. "An Index of Literary Materials in THE CRISIS, 1910-1934: Articles, Belles Lettres, and Book Reviews." CLA JOURNAL, 14 (1971), 452-65; 15 (1971), 197-234.

Although not primarily a literary journal, W.E.B. DuBois's NAACP publication printed a significant amount of literary material.

ESQUIRE, THE MAGAZINE FOR MEN (1933-current)

Beatty, Jerome, Jr. "Hemingway vs. ESQUIRE." SATURDAY REVIEW, 23 August 1958, pp. 9-11, 36.

Beatty discusses a suit brought by Hemingway's lawyer to prevent the republication in an anthology of three Spanish Civil War stories which first appeared in ESQUIRE in 1938 and 1939.

Grimes, Sister Richard Mary. "Hemingway: The Years with ESQUIRE." Dissertation, Ohio State University, 1965.

Hemingway submitted nonfiction articles, letters, and short stories to ESQUIRE from 1933 to 1936, and three more short stories in 1938 and 1939. His relationship with the periodical, including his departure from it, are examined.

Hagemann, E.R., and James E. Marsh. "Contributions of Literary Import to ESQUIRE, 1933-1941: An Annotated Check-List." BULLETIN OF BIBLIOGRAPHY, 22 (1957), 33-40, 69-72.

During the first eight years of ESQUIRE's existence, under the editorship of Arnold Gingrich, "there was published a surprising amount of excellent and high quality literature."

Hayes, Harold T.P. "Arnold Gingrich, ESQUIRE." NEW REPUBLIC, 4 September 1976, pp. 33-37.

Included in this portrait of ESQUIRE's first editor is information on his relationship with writers such as F. Scott Fitzgerald, Ernest Hemingway, and Norman Mailer.

Oberfirst, Robert. "Analysis of an ESQUIRE Short Short Story." WRITER, 57 (1944), 238-41.

This examination of "The Test of the Informer" by Jim Kjelgaard reveals that ESQUIRE's fiction is "strong and robust and contains fewer editorial taboos than any other popular American magazine fiction."

## THE HARVARD LAMPOON (1876-current)

Kaplan, Martin, comp. THE HARVARD LAMPOON CENTENNIAL CELEBRATION, 1876-1973. Boston: Little, Brown, 1973.

John Updike provides a foreword to this collection.

McCoy, Robert. "John Updike's Literary Apprenticeship on THE HARVARD LAMPOON." MODERN FICTION STUDIES, 20 (1974), 3-12.

Updike's "literary apprenticeship on THE HARVARD LAMPOON clearly sharpened his wit, his artist's descriptive eye, and his sense of the essential ambiguity of life. A measure of the impact of this indirect experience on his career may be taken from the astonishing quickness of his professional acceptance."

## THE LADIES' HOME JOURNAL (1883-current)

Oberfirst, Robert. "Analysis of a LADIES' HOME JOURNAL Short Stort Story." WRITER, 58 (1945), 382-85.

> Oberfirst analyzes Nancy Moore's "The Matinee," and among his conclusions is the following: "Most big time magazines are publishing short shorts which show a tendency toward simple, vital plots and better characterization."

## THE NATION (1865-current)

Green, Gordon C. "An Analytical Study of the Dramatic Criticism of Joseph Wood Krutch as Published in THE NATION, 1924-1952." Dissertation, University of Southern California, 1959.

> Green not only examines Krutch's criticism, but uses it to gain insight into the development of the Broadway theater during this period.

Hicks, Granville. "A 'Nation' Divided." GRANVILLE HICKS IN THE NEW MASSES. Ed. Jack Alan Robbins. Port Washington, N.Y.: Kennikat Press, 1974, pp. 302-9.

> Hicks attacks Joseph Wood Krutch, literary editor of the NATION from 1933 to 1937, and his successor Margaret Marshall for bias in the book review section against left-wing writers generally and Communists in particular. This article first appeared in the December 7, 1937, issue of the NEW MASSES.

Laing, Alexander. "THE NATION and Its Poets." NATION, 201 (1965), 212-18.

> This article discusses the quality and quantity of verse which appeared in the journal throughout its hundred-year history.

McFate, Patricia. "The Publication of James Stephens' Short Stories in 'The Nation.'" PAPERS OF THE BIBLIOGRAPHICAL SOCIETY OF AMERICA, 58 (1964), 476-77.

> McFate lists twelve stories published by Stephens in the NATION between December 1912 and January 1914.

Sterne, Richard Clark. "THE NATION and Its Century." NATION, 201 (1965), 42-53, 241-334.

> The following sections of this article discuss the journal's changing attitudes toward modern literary developments: "III: Literature and Ideas: 1865-1918" (pp. 274-82); "V: Literature and Ideas, 1918-

1933" (pp. 303-8); "VII: Literature and Ideas: 1933-1955" (pp. 325-32). The major shift in outlook by the NATION's editors and reviewers occurred in the early 1920's, when they moved from New Humanist views to an acceptance and praise of romanticism. From then on they were more interested in modern literary trends.

Van Doren, Carl. THREE WORLDS. New York: Harper and Brothers, 1936.

In "Journalism" (pp. 128-85), Van Doren relates some of his experiences while literary editor of the NATION after World War I. Included are discussions of the literary figures with whom he came in contact, including Ludwig Lewisohn, drama critic for the journal.

Van Doren, Mark. "The Personal Note: Mark Van Doren, Literary Editor: 1924-1928." NATION, 201 (1965), 35-36.

Van Doren reminisces about his editorship, including his experiences with contributors H.L. Mencken and Heywood Broun, among others.

THE NEW REPUBLIC (1914-current)

Bourke, Paul F. "The Status of Politics 1909-1919: THE NEW REPUBLIC, Randolph Bourne and Van Wyck Brooks." JOURNAL OF AMERICAN STUDIES, 8 (1974), 171-202.

In the course of studying the effect of World War I on American liberal political thought, Bourke traces the changing editorial outlook of the NEW REPUBLIC and Bourne's attacks on NEW REPUBLIC liberalism in the SEVEN ARTS.

Cowley, Malcolm. "A Reminiscence: Edmund Wilson on THE NEW REPUBLIC." NEW REPUBLIC, 1 July 1972, pp. 25-28.

Cowley remembers Wilson's work for the NEW REPUBLIC during the 1930's, first as an editor and then contributor. He compares this work to that done by Wilson for the NEW YORKER after 1940, following an argument and break with NEW REPUBLIC managing editor Bruce Bliven.

______. THINK BACK ON US . . . A CONTEMPORARY CHRONICLE OF THE 1930'S. Ed. Henry Dan Piper. Carbondale: Southern Illinois University Press, 1967; London: Feffer & Simons, 1967.

In "Epilogue: Adventures of a Book Reviewer" (pp. 385-92), Cowley describes his typical schedule while writing weekly book reviews for the NEW REPUBLIC. He notes that his copy was never altered and that editors Bruce Bliven and George Soule never suggested any controls over his work.

Munson, Gorham B. "Open Letter to the NEW REPUBLIC." SECESSION, no. 7 (Winter 1924), pp. 16-19.

Munson attacks the superficiality of some of the NEW REPUBLIC's literary criticism, and asks, "In perplexity at the confusion I have outlined . . . is it deliberately a showroom for all manner of critical writing, bad and good, for all kinds of approaches, exploded and tested?"

Test, George A[ustin]. "The NEW REPUBLIC as Little Magazine." AMERICAN QUARTERLY, 13 (1961), 189-92.

The NEW REPUBLIC has not been given enough credit for introducing new writers and important literature to the public, especially during Francis Hackett's reign as literary editor from 1914 to 1922.

_____. "The Vital Connection: A Study of THE NEW REPUBLIC Magazine as a Literary Journal, 1914-1922." Dissertation, University of Pennsylvania, 1960.

THE SATURDAY EVENING POST (1821-current)

Jeffery, Benjamin Miles. "The SATURDAY EVENING POST Short Story in the Nineteen-Twenties." Dissertation, University of Texas, 1966.

An examination of selected short stories reveals the conservative economic, social, and political views of editor George Horace Lorimer.

S., G. "THE SATURDAY EVENING POST." NEW REPUBLIC, 23 January 1915, p. 29.

The POST's fiction is criticized for its low quality.

Stevens, William J., Jr. "As the POST Likes It." THE WRITER'S HANDBOOK. Ed. A.S. Burack. Boston: The Writer, 1961, pp. 519-27.

The POST's assistant managing editor discusses the editorial preferences for fiction.

Tebbel, John. GEORGE HORACE LORIMER AND THE SATURDAY EVENING POST. Garden City, N.Y.: Doubleday, 1948.

Lorimer edited the POST from 1899 to 1936. His policies, some of which are described in chapters III and IV, "The POST School of Fiction" and "The POST School of Fiction: II," raised the periodical's circulation to more than two million.

# INDEX

This index includes authors, editors, and titles of books cited in the text. Alphabetization is letter by letter. Page references to sections on individual periodicals have been underlined.

## A

## B

## D

## E

## G

## J



## K



## L

## M

## N

## Q

## T

## W